Pg 24

IMPERIAL
LEGITIMATION

Uxori carissimae
patientissimae linguarum scienti

IMPERIAL LEGITIMATION

The Iconography of the Golden
Age Myth on Roman Imperial
Coinage of the Third Century AD

Graham Barker

SPINK

First published in 2020 by Spink and Son Ltd

Coin images on the cover are as follows:

Aureus of Septimius Severus (RIC IV 327) © Vienna Kunsthistorisches Museum: RÖ 1446

Aureus of Philip I (RIC IV 25a, p71) © British Museum: 1896,0608.59.

Aureus of Septimius Severus (RIC IV 274) © Roma Numismatics Auction 4, Lot 574, September 2012 https://www.romanumismatics.com

Engraving on the cover:

'*Jeux Séculaires*' by SD Mirys from *Figures de L'Histoire de la Republique Romaine*, 1799, Paris © Graham Barker (author's copy)

A CIP catalogue record for this book is available from the British Library.

ISBN 978-1-912667-47-5

Typeset by Russell Whittle

Printed and bound by Gutenberg Press Ltd, Malta

Spink and Son Ltd
69 Southampton Row
London WC1B 4ET

www.spinkbooks.com

CONTENTS

This medallion was produced to mark the Millennial Saecular Games celebrated in AD 248. The obverse has images of the Imperial Family: Philip I, his wife Otacilia Severa and son Philip II with the inscription CONCORDIA AVGVSTORVM (the harmony of the Augusti). The reverse depicts a sacrifice by Philip I and Philip II at a garlanded altar before an octostyle temple. Each emperor has two attendants while a central figure plays a double flute (*Aulos*). The reverse inscription is SAECVLVM NOVVM (the new age). © British Museum: 1872,0709.418.

FOREWORD

Written jointly by:
Richard Abdy, British Museum *Curator of Iron Age and Roman Coins*
Dr Sam Moorhead British Museum *National Finds Adviser for Iron Age and Roman coins Portable Antiquities and Treasure*

Many people will have become familiar with Rome's most flamboyant festival, the Saecular Games, through the fictionalised account in Robert Graves's sequel to his classic novel *I Claudius*. Graves has this most bookish of emperors engaged in convoluted research (contra to the Byzantine historian Zosimus's opinion) to ascertain the best time to revive the saecular games. Finally, in a triumphant highpoint of his reign – tempered by Graves's humour – he has Claudius write: "I had sent heralds out some months before to summon all citizens (in the old formula) 'to a spectacle which nobody now living has ever seen before, and which nobody now living shall ever see again'. This provoked a few sneers because Augustus's celebration of sixty-four years previously was remembered by a number of old men and women… " Graves understood the point of the games and its timing since it was made explicit in ancient literature: … *because the longest human lifespan is equal to the distance between successive occurrences of this festival, and the Romans call a lifetime a saeculum. It brings about cures of plagues, pestilence and diseases.* (Zosimus, *New History* 2, 1).

Ironically, amongst the emperors who celebrated Rome's Saecular Games, Claudius has left us with the least evidence of this event on his coinage. This book is in fact concerned with the legacy of the great festival as it is commemorated with some of the most beguiling and inventive coin types of the third century AD – just as Rome arrived at its final and most turbulent century as an officially pagan city. It would truly have been a heartfelt yearning for a lost Golden Age. To get us to this late epoch of Roman history it is worth returning to Zosimus (*New History* 2, 4-6) at length as he neatly brings us up to the Severan era from his vantage point some three centuries later:

> …*when disease and war beset them in the five hundred and fifth year after the foundation of the city (249 B.C.), the senate wished to find relief from these evils in the Sibylline oracles and ordered the Decemviri appointed for this purpose to consult them. The learned men prophesied that the calamity would cease if sacrifices were offered to Dis and Persephone, so they sought out the place again and sacrificed as directed[…]in the fourth consulship of Marcus Popillius (348 B.C.). When the sacrifice was complete and they had been delivered of their afflictions, the altar in some far corner of the Campus Martius was covered over again. This sacrifice was forgotten again for a long time until some misfortunes caused Octavian Augustus to renew the festival (17 B.C.) last held in the consulship of Lucius (Marcius) Censorinus and Manius Manilius (149 B.C.). Ateius Capito explained the law and the Quindecemviri appointed to keep the*

Sibylline oracles investigated the times at which the sacrifice was to be made and the games to be held. After Augustus, Claudius celebrated the festival without regard for the specified interval (A.D. 47), but then Domitian disregarded Claudius and calculated the cycle of years from the time when Augustus celebrated the festival, thus appearing to observe the original institution (A.D. 88). Severus, after another hundred and ten years celebrated the same festival with his sons, Antoninus (Carcacalla) and Geta in the consulship of Chilo and Libo (A.D. 204).

This is how we are told the festival was celebrated. Heralds go about summoning everyone to attend a spectacle they have never seen before and will never see again. In summer, a few days before it begins, the Quindecemviri sit in the Capitol and in the Palatine temple on a tribunal and distribute purifying agents, such as torches, brimstone and pitch, to the people; slaves do not participate in this, only freemen. When all the people assemble in the above-mentioned places and in the temple of Diana on the Aventine, each one bringing wheat, barley and beans, they keep the all-night vigils to the Fates with great solemnity... Then when the time arrives for the festival, which is celebrated for three days and three nights in the Campus Martius, the victims are dedicated on the bank of the Tiber at Tarentum. They sacrifice to Jupiter, Juno, Apollo, Latona, Diana, and also to the Fates, Lucina, Ceres, Dis and Proserpine. On the first night of the spectacle, at the second hour, the emperor with the Quindecemviri sacrifices three lambs on three altars on the riverbank, and sprinkling the altars with blood, he offers up the victims burnt whole. After preparing a stage like that in a theatre, they light torches and a fire, sing a newly composed song, and present sacred spectacles. Those who participate are rewarded with the first fruits of the wheat, barley and beans, for they are distributed to all the people, as I said. The next day they go up to the Capitol where they offer the usual sacrifices, and thence to the theatre where games to Apollo and Diana are celebrated. On the second day noble ladies, gathering at the Capitol at the place specified by the oracle, pray to and sing the praises of the goddess, as is right. On the third day in the temple of Apollo on the Palatine, twenty seven outstanding boys and as many girls, all of whom have two living parents, sing hymns and victory songs in both Greek and Latin for the preservation of the Roman empire. There were other celebrations as well, in accordance with the gods' direction, and as long as they were all observed, the Roman Empire remained intact. To convince us of the truth in these matters, I will add the Sibyl's oracle although others before me have already referred to it.

"When the longest span of human life has elapsed,
And the cycle of years comes round to one hundred and ten,
Remember Romans, especially if you are forgetful,
Remember all this, to the immortal gods…"

Graham Barker has skilfully woven together literary, archaeological and numismatic sources to create a rich tapestry for the Saecular Games in the 3rd century AD. Although embedded in Rome's earlier history, he shows how the tradition of the Saecular Games takes on its own distinct character in the later Roman period. It is a time of political and military turmoil, but also one of religious and philosophical change and this book skilfully intertwines the different elements into a cogent and informative narrative. The *Appendices* offer texts of Virgil's *Eclogue* IV, Horace's *Carmen Saeculare* (the hymn of the Saecular Games) and an extract from Ovid's *Metamorphorses* Book I; Appendix IV presents a reconstructed account of the Saecular Games of AD 204, deftly crafted from ancient sources by an author who is much in tune with the world of drama and ceremony. It often needs people with other experiences to ignite sparks of originality in numismatics!

Finally, this book places numismatics centre-stage, showing how, if used as historical sources, coins can illuminate a great deal about Roman history and culture. Fittingly, the reader will find this work lavishly illustrated with 170 images – all necessary to cover the rich visual language the Saecular games inspired. A feast for the modern eyes just as the subject was so clearly a feast for the pagan soul.

Table of Figures

Note: the coins illustrated show the relative size of each denomination but this is approximate and smaller coins are enlarged for greater clarity.

LIST OF TABLES

ACKNOWLEDGEMENTS

This book developed from my Master's thesis at the University of Warwick in 2016. My sincere thanks are due to my tutor Kevin Butcher and all his colleagues at the Department of Classsics and Ancient History, with special thanks to Clare Rowan. I am greatly indebted to the inspiration and encouragement from Sam Moorhead and Richard Abdy at the British Museum. I am especially grateful to Sam Moorhead and my wife, Joanna, for proof reading the entire script. I would like to thank Roger Bland and his colleagues at the Royal Numismatic Society for suggesting publication in the first place and the indefatigable Emma Howard at Spink for agreeing to publish this monograph. I also owe a great debt to Russ Whittle at Spink for his tireless assistance with the publication. For a wide range of assistance with text and illustrations I am grateful to the following: the Trustees of the British Museum, Richard Beale, Stephanie Boonstra, Karsten Dahmen, Emma Dodd, Vincent Drost, Sylviane Estiot, Carolin Goll, Arcangela Carbone Gross, Harvard University Press, Johan van Heesch, Chris Howgego, Adam Kline, Florian Kugler, Dane Kurth, Simon Leuthi, Jerome Mairat, Eric McFadden, Mounzer Nazha, David Miller, Oxford University Press, Hadrien Rambach, Sam Moorhead, Elena Stolyarik, Max Tursi, Klaus Vendrovec. All errors are entirely my own.

LIST OF ABBREVIATIONS

CHRB   Coin Hoards from Roman Britain (1975). London.

CIL   *Corpus Inscriptionum Latinarum* (1863). Berlin.

CIMRM   Vermaseren, M. (1956 and 1960) *Corpus Inscriptionum et Monumentorum Religionis Mithriacae*. The Hague.

ILS   Dessau, H., *Inscriptiones Latinae Selectae* (1892). Berlin.

LIMC   *Lexicon Iconographicum Mythologiae Classicae* (1981). Zurich.

P. Oxy   Grenfell, B. and Hunt, A. The Oxyrhynchus Papyri. (1898). London.

RIB   Collingwood, R and Wright, R. (1965) Roman Inscriptions of Britain. Oxford.

RIC   Roman Imperial Coinage. 1923 - 2019. London.

SHA   *Scriptores Historiae Augustae*.

INTRODUCTION

"Who does not know of the Golden Age of the untroubled king?"[1]

This line, from the poem *Aetna*, was probably written in the mid first century AD. The unknown author indicates that the Golden Age myth was so well-known that, by this time, it had become a common-place theme. The origins of the myth can be traced back to Hesiod, and a brief history of the Golden Age myth, its development and its reshaping during the reign of Augustus, is discussed below. It is perhaps not surprising that the myth seems to have continued to evolve over time to suit various needs and purposes. [2]

Under Augustus, it was claimed that a new Golden Age was ushered in by performing sacred rituals at the Saecular Games, sanctioned by a Sybilline Oracle.[3] The Augustan Saecular Games of 17 BC have been described as "one of most the most spectacular religious celebrations ever seen." [4] While Augustus is seen as a great "reinventer of tradition," [5] it can be argued that, in terms of a renewal of the population of Rome, these rituals served as "a reconnection of the Augustan State rite to earlier antecedents." [6] Above all, the Augustan Saecular Games can clearly be seen as part of a programme of legitimation by the emperor, following the bitter divisions caused by civil war.[7] The three days of specified rituals were followed by seven days of games, races, plays, dances, military and hunting displays.[8] They were commemorated by a vast marble inscription,[9] much of which survives. Coins were issued with specific iconography and an inscription recording the fact that the Games had taken place. Just as the act of inscribing the details of the games in marble may have formed part of sacred rituals, so the production and distribution of coins with the dated *cippus* also probably formed part of the religious ceremonies.[10] The issue of coinage with this specific iconography would be repeated by several later emperors who celebrated the Saecular Games, demonstrating a

---

1   *"Aurea securi quis nescit saecula regis"*, line 9, (translation by G Barker).

2   Forsyth, 2012, 73; Barker, 1996, 436.

3   Zosimus, *Historia Nova*, 2.6; For the oracle recorded by Phlegon of Tralles see: Hansen, 1996, 56. For the rituals and games see: Beard, 1998, s5.7b; Rantala, 2013, 55-148.

4   Miller, 2009, 253.

5   Flower, 2014, 286; Sobocinski, 2006, 584; Galinsky,1996, 102; Zanker, 1998, 167; Scott Ryberg, 1958, 112-131; cf. Suetonius who describes Augustus as a "reviver of ancient rites" (including the Saecular Games): Suetonius, Life of Augustus, 31.3.

6   Habinek, 2005,152. See also the more recent statement that Augustus invoked earlier initiatives as a means of anchoring innovation: Morrell, Osgood & Welch, 2019, 13.

7   Lovatt, 2016, 362; Rantala, 2013, 19. On orthopraxy in roman religion see Scheid, 2005, 348ff.

8   Beard, North, Price, 1998,143-144.

9   CIL, vol. VI, 32,323, 50-63, 90-168; Schnegg-Kohler, 2002.

10 Rowan, 2012, 64; see Beard, 1985,114 on this concept for the Arval acta.

remarkable numismatic consistency of design for this type of coin across the centuries.[11]

On the reverse of a dated Augustan *denarius* (Figure 1) can be found the inscription XV – SF, on either side of the *cippus,* which is a reference to the *quindecemviri sacris faciundis* (the high council of the fifteen officials for sacred affairs), the priestly college of an elite group of men, including the emperor, responsible for the Sybilline books, the regulation of foreign cults and the Saecular Games.[12]

Figure 1: Denarius of Augustus: (RIC I 354) © British Museum: 2002,0102.4968

Such was the power of the Augustan Saecular Games and the Golden Age mythology, set down by the leading writers of the day, that many subsequent emperors sought to emulate the precedent set by Augustus. [13] For example, Claudius celebrated the Saecular Games in AD 47,[14] although no coin issues are known, and Domitian celebrated the Games in AD 88 with a spectacular series of coins[15] to mark the event, including a dated *cippus* coin (Figure 2).

Figure 2: Denarius of Domitian: (RIC II 604) © CNG Auction 91, Lot 88 September 2012

Using the evidence of numismatic iconography, this book sets out to explore the extent to which Roman emperors of the third century AD followed the

11 Rowan, 2012, 60-65.
12 Johnston (ed.), 2004 636; Adkins, 1996, 188.
13 Mattingly, 1947, 18.
14 Tacitus, *Annales*, XI.11; Censorinus, *De Die Natali*, XVII; CIL VI 32324; Pighi, 1941, 131-132.
15 RIC II part 1 595 – 628.

Augustan precedent and claimed a new Golden Age. For the Severan period, relevant iconography from the late second century has been included. The aim of the book is to set coin iconography, where possible, in the context of relevant written sources and contemporary Roman art.[16] While the aim is to discuss and illustrate the majority of known examples of coinage, the writings and images chosen here are selectively drawn for illustration and are not intended to be exhaustive. Where appropriate, iconography is traced to numismatic sources before the third century AD to illustrate the development of an image. Some examples from the fourth century AD of key images are also shown to illustrate the continuity of iconography beyond the third century AD.

The debate about the interpretation of coin iconography and the extent to which coins were imperial messages has long been the subject of discussion.[17] The principles of literary theory help to lend caution over the interpretation of inscriptions, texts and images from classical times.[18] In recent years, perhaps, more writers have come to the view that coins were important vehicles for the dissemination of imperial ideals.[19] Most of the coins examined in this book, though not all, were issued in small numbers with a limited circulation. The possible reasons for this are discussed below. Nonetheless, it is contended here that the iconography depicted on coinage illustrates an imperial claim to a returning Golden Age which, in the maelstrom of religious ideas and associated writings of the third century AD, became a recurring theme of legitimation for many emperors. The fourth century AD was to see a continued emphasis on particular Golden Age themes but, by this time, chiefly in a Christian context.

The Golden Age Myth

The utopian dream of returning to a time of perfect peace, or "paradise lost", exists in many ancient mythologies.[20] In terms of the antecedents to the Roman version of the myth, Hesiod is the first author to make reference to it, though the early myth centred on the concept of a succession of races.[21] In Hesiod's version (c. 700 BC) there are five ages: the iron age, the age of heroes, the bronze age, the silver age, the golden age.[22] The development of the myth following Hesiod is complex.[23] Plato wrote about the Golden Age [24] and his writings, along with those of Empedocles, the Orphics and the Stoics, developed the concept of

---

16 Elkins, 2009, 29; Krmnicek and Elkins, 2014, 9; Howgego, 2014, 17.

17 Burnett, 1987, 90-92; Noreña, 2001, 146-148; Wallace-Hadrill, 1986, 66-87; Howgego and Heuchert, 2005; Sobocinski, 2006, 581- 602; Rowan, 2013, 211-246.

18 Martindale, 1993, 1-29; Kennedy, 1992,26-58.

19 Noreña, 2001, 268.

20 Eliade, 1949, 6-48; Feeney, 2007, 109-115; Strootman, 2014, 325.

21 Evans, 2008, 34.

22 Hesiod, Works and Days, 109-201.

23 Gee, 2013, 36-56; Vidal-Naquet, 1978, 132-141.

24 Plato, The Statesman, 268d -274e.

cyclical time returning man to a former state of bliss.[25] The Etruscans believed in a series of *saecula* which would define the end of Etruscan civilisation.[26] The works of Aratus were translated by Cicero and Germanicus, amongst others, and are key to the development of the Roman version of the myth.[27]

The first Roman writer to refer to the myth was Varro (116-27 BC).[28] His writings came at a time when, it has been argued, an intellectual elite sought to codify Roman religious practice.[29] Cicero (106 – 43 BC) referred to astrological aspects of the Golden Age myth when he wrote:

> *"On the diverse motions of the planets, the mathematicians have based what they call the Great Year which is completed when the sun, moon and five planets having all finished their course have returned to the same positions relative to one another."* [30]

Astrology, which came to prominence in Rome at the end of the Republic,[31] was central to the cyclical concept of the Golden Age myth. Augustus exploited the S*idus Iulium* (the star of Julius Caesar) to promote the apotheosis of Caesar, the prophetic nature of the dynasty and the coming of the Golden Age.[32] The *Sidus Iulium,* for example, featured on the herald's shield at the Saecular Games according to numismatic evidence (Figure 3). The *sidus* also appears on the obverse above the head of the deified Caesar.

Suetonius wrote of an episode when Augustus adopted the sign of Capricorn at a horoscope reading and went on to employ the emblem on his silver coinage.[33] Capricorn can be interpreted as a sign ruling over the dawning of new Golden age and astrology was clearly part of the imperial rhetoric.[34] The relationship between the exercise of power and astrology has been summed up as follows: "It was, in large measure, astrology that provided, in the Roman period, the grammar and vocabulary for articulating power concepts." [35]

---

25   Aratus, *Phaenomena*, 96-136; Gee, 2013, 81-109.

26   Santangelo, 2013, 118; Feeney, 2007, 146; De Grummond, 2006, 31; Censorinus, *De Die Natali*, 17.5-6.

27   Gee, 2013, 48.

28   Varro, *De Re Rustica,* 3.1.5.

29   Macrae, 2016, 55.

30   *Quarum ex disparibus motionibus magnum annum mathematici nominaverunt, qui tum efficitur, cum solis et lunae et quinque errantium ad eandem inter se comparationem confectis omnium spatiis est facta conversio.* Cicero, *De Natura Deorum*, 2.51 (translation by H. Rackham).

31   Barton, 1994, 38; Aratus, *Phaenomena*.

32   Williams, 2003, 1-29.

33   Suetonius, Augustus, 94.12; Augustus was born on 23 September and therefore under the zodiacal sign of Libra; perhaps Augustus was conceived under Capricorn but this is not known for certain.

34   Barton, 1995, 48; Capricorn and the *Sidus Iulium* appear on the *Gemma Augustea* (see Figure 116).

35   Oster, 1982, 203.

Figure 3: Denarius of Augustus: (RIC I 340) © British Museum: 1860,0330.23

Many Roman writers wrote about the Golden Age myth but the poet most closely associated with articulating the Augustan Golden Age is Virgil (70 BC - 19 BC). Key references can be found in the *Aeneid*, the *Georgics* and the *Eclogues*. Whilst the concept of cyclical time had never been far away from the myth, the principle of a returning Golden Age first appears in Virgil.[36] In Virgil's version, the tutelary deity becomes Saturn rather than Cronus.[37] In another Augustan redefinition, Virgil also prescribes that the peace of the Golden Age is attained through agricultural labour.[38] The Augustan Golden Age, achieved through victory in war,[39] brought about peace, prosperity and a new morality.[40]

One aspect of the myth that occurs again and again, throughout the Roman imperial period, is the potential decline from a happy Golden Age to one of iron and rust.[41] The function of the implicit fear which stemmed from a potential fall into disorder was "to put the emperor at the centre of the scheme of things".[42] In the *Aeneid*, Anchises makes a prophecy in these terms:

"Augustus Caesar, offspring of a god, who will again found an Age of Gold in Latium across fields which were once ruled by Saturn" [43]

The presentation of Augustus as the messianic figure at the centre of a new Saturnian Golden Age is articulated in Virgil's Fourth Eclogue:

"Now is come the last age of Cumaean song; the great line of the centuries begins anew. Now the Virgin returns, the reign of Saturn returns; now a new generation descends from heaven on high. Only do you, pure Lucina, smile on the birth of the child, under whom the iron

---

36 Gee, 2013, 39.

37 Galinsky, 1996, 95. The cult of Saturn followed the Greek rite: Versnel, 1993, 139.

38 Virgil, Georgics II, 536-40; Galinsky, 1996, 121; Johnston, 1980.

39 Galinsky, 1996, 107; Augustus, *Res Gestae*, 13: *parta victoriis pax* (peace through victory).

40 Forsyth, 2012, 71.

41 See for example Suetonius, Tiberius, 59; Cassius Dio, *Historia Romana*, LXXII.36.4.

42 Wallace-Hadrill, 1982, 25; Satterfield, 2016, 325.

43 *"Augustus Caesar, divi genus, aurea condet/ Saecula qui rursus Latio regnata per arva/ Saturno quondam."* Virgil, *Aeneid* VI, 792-794 (translation by G. Barker).

brood shall at last cease and a golden race spring up throughout the world! Your own Apollo now is king!" [44]

This appeal for a nostalgic return, following a time of crisis and uncertainty, is based on an attempt to establish a "deep legitimacy." [45] The depth of this legitimacy has been expressed as: "a mythical reality outside ours...lying beyond the borders of history and space, an eternal truth that existed before time but still exists behind it and behind our reality". [46]

Another strand to establishing legitimacy was an appeal to *mos maiorum* (custom of the ancestors). [47] This has been defined as "time honoured principles, traditional models and rules of appropriate conduct". [48] Before celebrating the Saecular Games, Augustus implemented an extraordinary legislative programme on morals and marriage, later described as *exempla maiorum* (exemplary ancestral practices). [49] The laws were there to ensure the Golden Age was a new age of morality and the Saecular Games could then usher in a moral rebirth of Rome. [50]

Part of the Republican legacy, also seized on by Augustus for legitimisation purposes, was dynastic continuity. [51] When Julius Caesar made Octavian his heir Augustus inherited the loyalty of Caesar's soldiers and supporters. The promise of a Golden Age continuing with a dynastic successor became "a topos in panegyrical literature." [52] Despite repeated failures in Roman imperial history, the desire for dynastic continuity remained strong and linked to the myth of Golden Age.

The last line of the above quotation from Virgil's Fourth Eclogue emphasises that Apollo is the symbol of the new age. [53] Augustus cultivated Apollo all his life and Suetonius records that he was born on 23 September, [54] the Festival of Apollo. [55] The *Carmen Saeculare*, specially commissioned for the Saecular Games from Horace, is a hymn which emphasises the role of Apollo and his sister Diana. In their respective roles as deities associated with the sun

---

44   Virgil, *Eclogue* IV, 5-10 (translation by H. Fairclough); for the Latin see Appendix I; the verb *condere* can also mean 'to see the end of' as well as 'to found' but Virgil's line should only be seen as adulatory: Zanker, 2010, 498.

45   Versnel, 1994, 119.

46   Weidkuhn, 1977, 174.

47   Sommer, 2011, 167.

48   Holkëskamp, 2010, 17.

49   *Res Gestae Divi Augustus*, 8.5 (translation by Cooley).

50   Rantala, 2013,13; Galinsky, 1996, 100-106, 128-138.

51   Sommer, 2011, 177.

52   Versnel, 1993, 205; e.g. Ovid, Metamorphoses, 15.835.

53   Miller, 2009, 253ff.

54   Suetonius, *Augustus*, 94.5.

55   Feeney, 2007, 154.

and moon, they can be seen as a cosmic metaphor for eternity.[56] The absence of a specific Golden Age reference in the Carmen Saeculare has attracted comment.[57] Yet Horace's hymn is essentially about the eternal continuity of the *saecula*[58] and also reflects Augustus' new age of morality[59] along with the alteration of the traditional rituals of atonement into a celebration of the new age of peace and prosperity.[60] Horace made specific reference the Golden Age of Augustus elsewhere:

> *"He whom no blessing more sublime*
> *Or good the bounteous Gods did e'er accord,*
> *Or Fates to earth, nor will, though were restored*
> *The Golden Age of earlier Time."* [61]

It seems most likely that Horace was avoiding the complexities of unrealistic claims and conflicting traditions of the Golden Age.[62] What is clear is that the performance of Horace's words by 27 girls and 27 boys[63] was an integral part of the Saecular Games rituals: "there is no secular rite without the *Carmen Saeculare*: actions and words are co-constructive of the ritual".[64]

A clear description of the Roman cyclical concept of the four ages is found in Ovid (43 BC - AD 17).[65] The four ages came to encapsulate the *magnus annus* (great year) which is referenced in the quotation by Cicero above. In turn the four ages came to be represented by the four seasons in Roman iconography.[66] In *De Die Natali* (the Natal Day), by Censorinus, a scholar of the third century AD, the time frame of the *magnus annus* is said to vary greatly (*magnitudo adeo diversa etiam gentibus observata quam auctoribus tradita est*).[67] Pliny (AD 23-AD 79), citing his contemporary Manilius, suggests a period of 540 years which was thought to be the lifespan of the Phoenix.[68] The *magnus annus*

---

56   Hijmans, 2009, 566; see Appendix II for the full text and translation.

57   Barker, 1996, 426; Zanker, 2010, 495-516.

58   Hijmans, 564; for intertextuality between the *Carmen Saeculare* and the Fourth *Eclogue* see *Barker*, 1996, 438 and Whittaker, 2007, 76.

59   Horace *Carmen Saeculare*, 17-20; see Appendix II.

60   Miller, 2009, 253.

61   *quo nihil maius meliusve terries/ fata donavere bonique divi/ nec dabunt, quamvis redeant in aurum/ tempora priscum*; Horace, Odes Book IV, II, 37-44 (translation M Harris). See also Horace, Epode xvi 63-66.

62   Zanker, 2010, 496.

63   Three was a sacred number (27=3x3x3); Sybilline oracles had a history of requiring choirs of 27 children: Poe,1984,63.

64   Habinek, 2005, 152

65   Ovid, *Metamorphoses*, 1.89-150. See Appendix III.

66   Pollini, 1992, 296. Manilius, *Astronomica*, 2.398 - 405; Censorinus, *De Die Natali*, XVIII, 35ff.

67   Censorinus, *De Die Natali*, XVIII, 1-2.

68   Pliny, *Historia Naturalis*, X.2.

is discussed below in Chapter 5.3 in the context of the iconography of the Phoenix.

The works of Calpurnius Siculus have been variously dated to the reign of Nero, to a post-Neronian period or to the third century AD. [69] His first *Eclogue* includes the line:

" A Golden Age will be reborn bringing security and peace" [70]

Censorinus, who is thought to have written in the third century AD, largely based *De Die Natali* on the writings of Varro (116 BC – c.27 BC), who is frequently quoted throughout the work.[71] This elaborate speech is essentially a tribute to his patron, Quintius Caerelius, on his birthday. He discusses various aspects of time and, following a reference to the Golden Age,[72] he includes a section on the Saecular Games and describes its Etruscan origins. Citing Varro, he makes distinction between two types of *saecula*: natural and civil. A natural *saeculum* is described as *spatium vitae humanae longissimum partu et morte definitum* (the longest duration of human life having for its limits the birth and death of man).[73] Censorinus cites various periods for the length of a *saeculum* and frequently mentions 100 years.[74] Horace, in the *Carmen Saeculare*, clearly cites 110 years[75] which chimes with period mentioned in the Sybilline Oracle quoted by Phlegon of Tralles[76] and Zosimus. [77] It has been suggested that there may have been two competing traditions of a *saeculum* lasting 100 or 110 years with Augustus siding with the latter. [78]

Censorinus refers to the Etruscan origins of the *saeculum,* which varied greatly in the number of years, and goes on to say that a Roman *saeculum* is not fixed and that the truth is hidden and obscure (*veritas in obscuro latet*).[79] It may be that this refers to a distinction between the natural or Sybilline *saeculum* which was not a fixed number of years while the civil *saeculum* lasted for either 100 or 110 years. [80] The civil *saeculum* came to have direct reference to the anniversary of the foundation of Rome. This important text is thought to date

---

69   Champlin, 1978, 95-110; Feeney, 2007, 136.

70   *"aurea secura cum pace renascitur aetas"* (line 42); translation by G Barker.

71   O'Mara, 2003, 17-26.

72   Censorinus, *De Die Natali*, XVI, 7.

73   Censorinus, *De Die Natali*, XVII, 1 (translation by W. Maude) ; Luke, 2014 ,224.

74   In the *Res Gestae* of Augustus 100 years is also mentioned: Cooley, 2009, 85 (Chapter 22). See Wiseman, 2019, 108.

75   Horace, *Carmen Saeculare*, 21; Appendix II.

76   For the oracle recorded by Phlegon of Tralles in Hadrian's reign, see: Hansen, 1996, 56.

77   Zosimus, *Historia Nova*, 2.6.

78   Santangelo, 2013, 118; Lipka, 2009, 154..

79   The Etruscan concept of successive ages was clearly complex: Santangelo, 2013, 117.

80   Santangelo, 2013, 120.

from AD 238 and can be seen as testimony to the enduring prominence of the Golden Age myth and the Saecular Games in the third century AD.[81]

Overview of the history of the Saecular Games

Censorinus states that the Augustan Saecular Games were the fifth to be celebrated and he lists the preceding Games, while recording different traditions in dating the early Games.[82] The origins of the Saecular Games, including its Etruscan antecedents, can only be pieced together from fragments of different writers, some of which are contradictory. One of the main functions of the Games was purificatory and key preparatory rituals for the Games included lustral rites.[83] Censorinus refers to an obscure author called Valerius Antias and quotes him several times as well as Varro in detailing the history and dates of the Republican Saecular Games, which may originally have been known as the Tarentine Games, whose emphasis was the expiation of prodigies. [84]

A certain Valerius Maximus, writing in the reign of Tiberius, provides what has been called the 'charter myth' of the Saecular Games and also probably drew on Valerius Antias. [85] The myth was also later recorded by Zosimus. [86] This is the myth of Valesius whose three children were struck with down with the plague. Valesius is told by the gods that the children will be saved if they are given water from the altar of Dis and and Proserpina[87] at the Tarentum. The three children are duly cured. Valesius then receives divine instruction to conduct specified sacrifices at the altar, to hold *lectisternia* (ritual banquets) and to celebrate games on three consecutive days. The myth may indicate that the Saecular Games were originally intended to protect the Roman population, and children in particular, from epidemics. Alongside the birth of a new *saeculum* the rituals emphasised protection for the safe birth of children in the new era.[88]

Valerius Maximus also mentions that Valerius Publicola followed the rituals which were followed at the start of the Republic. Plutarch tells us that these first Games were held in 504 BC,[89] after consulting the Sybilline books about a plague of miscarriages.[90] Censorinus writes that the date of the first Games was either 509 or 456 BC. [91] Plutarch also relates that Valerius Publicola is descended from an early Roman leader called Valerius and it may

81   Gordon, 1983, 226.

82   Santangelo, 2013, 118; Rantala, 2017, 193.

83   Galinsky, 2007,77; Luke, 2014, 223; Poe, 1984, 59.

84   Santangelo, 2013, 119; Valerius Maximus, *Fac. et dict. Memorabilium,* II.4.5; Censorinus, *De Die Natali,* XVII.

85   Forsythe, 2012, 49-50; Valerius Maximus, *Fact. et dict. Memorabilium,* II.4.5.

86   Zosimus, *Historia Nova,* 2.

87   Proserpina's myth incorporates the idea of rebirth: Forsyth, 2012, 63; Whittaker, 2007, 70.

88   Lipka, 2009, 165; Rantala, 2017, 66.

89   In the year Publicola was consul for the fourth time.

90   Plutarch, *Life of Publicola,* 21.1.

91   Censorinus, *De Die Natali,* XVII.

be inferred that, in turn, he can be identified with Valesius of the 'Charter myth'.[92] Therefore, through Valerius Publicola, the great Roman family of the Valerii are closely associated with the founding of the Saecular Games. Indeed, Valerius Maximus reports that the Tarentine Games were celebrated solely by the Valerian family until the state celebration of the Games in 249 BC.[93]

The early celebration of the the Saecular Games seem to have been closely linked to lightning strikes as prodigies requiring expiation.[94] Zosimus refers to lightning striking a grove a trees in the charter myth.[95] Varro is quoted by Censorinus in saying that in 249 BC the portent, which led to the consultation of the Sybilline books, was a bolt of lightning (the fire of heaven) striking a tower on the walls of Rome.[96] The Temple of Palatine Apollo, a key venue in the Augustan and later Saecular Games, was built on land which had been struck by lightning.[97] The same temple also housed the sacred Etruscan books on lightning. [98] A lightning strike was recorded as one of the events which led to the consultation of the Sybilline Books for the Augustan Saecular Games in 17 BC.[99] It is notable, in this context, that one of the ritual venues specified in the Augustan *Commentarii* was the temple of Jupiter the Thunderer, a temple also built by Augustus.[100] Arnobius records that the god Dis had the power to expiate thunderbolts which may explain his inclusion in the rituals of the Saecular Games. [101]

Censorinus dates the second Games as either 346 or 344 BC; although modern scholarship has suggested 362 BC is a more likely date.[102] The date of the third Games, when they probably came to be regarded by Romans as essential for the new *saeculum,* is generally agreed as 249 BC[103] though Censorinus also mentions a tradition that they were held in 236 BC. A writer from the time of Augustus, Verrius Flaccus, is quoted by a later writer, known as Pseudo Acro, confirming the date of 249 BC; he also records that the reason

92   Plutarch, *Life of Publicola,* 1.
93   Forsythe, 2012, 51; Habinek, 2005, 151; Coarelli, 1993, 211-45.
94   Poe, 1984, 59; Lipka, 2009, 157; see De Grummond, 1990, 39 for lightning in Etruscan lore;
95   Zosimus, 2.1.2: see the Foreword, page VII, for dates cited by Zosimus.
96   Censorinus, *De Die Natali,* XVII.8; Pighi, 1941, 67- 72.
97   Dio, 49.15.5; Suetonius, Aug. 29.3; Hekster, O. and Rich, J. , 2006, 151; Luke, 2014,162.
98   Servius, *In Vergilii Aeneidem commentarii,* 6.72.
99   This prodigy may have been fabricated: Satterfield, 2016, 325.
100   Augustan Commentarii (CIL 32323-4). The temple was built following Augustus' narrow escape from a lightning strike in northern Spain: Suetonius, Aug. 29.3.
101   Arnobius, *Adversus Nationes,* 5.37.
102   Forsythe, 2012, 55-57: Zosimus 2, 4-6, cites 348 BC.
103   Lipka, 2009, 148.

for holding the Saecular Games is to ensure success in the war against the Carthaginians [104] and that this was the time of the first Punic war. [105]

Censorinus gives three possible dates for the fourth Games: 149 BC, 146 BC and 126 BC. A series of victories by the Roman army in Africa and Greece in 146 BC makes this the more likely date.

In the first century BC, Sulla can be seen as the first in a series of men who presented themselves as the "man of the *saeculum*" or "a savior figure who was appointed by the gods and could bring an end to the great struggles of the age."[106] As the Saecular Games developed, they came to mark the transition from one *saeculum* to another, a critical event requiring rituals of purification.[107]

The date of the Augustan Saecular Games in 17 BC has been the cause of much speculation. However, in addition to recorded prodigies requiring expiation, it has been pointed out this year followed the repossession of the military standards from the Parthians, the passing of *Lex Iulia* by way of moral reforms, and also marked the tenth anniversary of Octavian's accepting the title Augustus. [108] Above all, there was the birth of Lucius Caesar, son of Marcus Agrippa, who may be another candidate for the child in the Fourth *Eclogue*.[109]

The Augustan Saecular Game emphasised a rebirth not only of a new order but of Rome itself.[110] Several elements of the Ludi Saeculares emphasised aspects of Rome's mythical birth. These elements included: the *Suffimenta* or purification ritual which echoed the ancient ceremonies of the *Parilia* on Rome's birthday and one of locations for the ritual was the *Roma Quadrata* said to be the site of Romulus's first settlement;[111] the *fruges* or 'First Fruits' ceremony which has a parallel with a ritual performed by Romulus at the founding of Rome when he put first fruits into a circular trench[112] and the *Lusus Troiae* (Trojan War Games) which recalls the mythical Trojan origins of Rome.[113] It may be that Augustus also intended to draw on the mystical Greek idea of palingenesis which concerned rebirth of the human soul. [114]

It has already been noted that, after Augustus, the Saecular Games were celebrated in AD 47 by the emperor Claudius to mark the 800th anniversary of Rome; though the evidence from coinage is slight. [115] However, when Domitian

104 Pighi, 1941, 59 – 66; Forsythe, 2012, 60.

105 Luke, 2014, 224; Luke suggests it is possible these Games aimed to cultivate ties with *Magna Graecia*.

106 Luke, 2014,17.

107 Luke, 2014, 224.

108   nie ewski, 2007, 113.

109 Luke, 2014, 226.

110 Luke, 2014, 225.

111 Plutarch, Life of Romulus. 11; Pighi, 1941, 146; Forsyth, 2012, 74-75.

112 Plutarch, Life of Romulus. 11; Ovid, *Fasti* IV. 89; t

113 Virgil, *Aeneid*, Book V, 545-603: see Appendix IV.

114 Luke, 2014, 224.

115 Tacitus, *Annales*, XI.11; Suetonius, *De Vita Caesarum*, 21.

celebrated the Games in AD 88, presumably as a 'natural' or Sybilline event, an extraordinary range of coinage was issued which depict a range of key rituals in the *Ludi Saeculares*.[116] It is probable that Antoninus Pius celebrated the Saecular Games for the 900th anniversary of Rome though the evidence is sparse.[117] This book covers in detail the Saecular Games of Septimius Severus in AD 204 and the Millennial Games of Philip in AD 248 which were officially the last to be recorded.

The way in which the Roman State marked the end of one *saeculum* and the start of a new *saeculum* with the rituals and ceremonies of the *ludi saeculares* can be seen as a powerful way of mastering the concept of time itself.[118] It has been commented that when the emperor Constantine chose not to celebrate the *Ludi Saeculares* in AD 314, principally on Christian grounds, this was a symbolic rupture of great power.[119]

Background to the Third Century AD

What crisis?

The problems of the third century AD have been the subject of detailed analysis.[120] Some major changes were instituted by emperors such as the extension of citizenship by the *constitutio antoniniana*, the decree of AD 212 in the reign of Caracalla.[121] Overall, the general tone of contemporary historians was deeply pessimistic.[122] Historians of the eighteenth century catalogued the range of issues facing the rulers of the Roman Empire at this time and, to a large extent, shaped the view of a "third century crisis".[123] More recent research suggests that different parts of Roman society in the third century AD were exposed to different problems and threats at different times.[124] Some of the major issues can be classified in three main categories.[125]

Firstly, the external threats to the borders of the empire reached unprecedented levels. As a consequence, the third century witnessed two

---

116 RIC II 595 - 628; Sobocinski, 2006, 581-602; see Foreword for Zosimus' opinion on the date.

117 Levick, 2014, 102; Whetstone,1978, 25; Aurelius Victor, *De Caesaribus*, 15.4. See the medallions issued by Antoninus Pius on myths of Rome e.g Gnecchi, 1912, II p 20/97 and coin issues such as RIC III 309.

118 Habinek, 2005, 150; Feeney, 2007, 147; though see Eliade, 1954, 134 for the fear that accompanied a new *Saeculum;* compare, perhaps, the modern day computer panic, known as Y2K, when approaching AD 2000.

119 Feeney, 2007, 147; Feeney comments that the new Christian era had its own way of ensuring it survived *per saecula saeculorum*.

120 MacMullen 1976; Alföldy 1975; Watson, 1999, 1-20; Dodds, 1965.

121 Du Plessis, 2015, 103; Ando, 2012, 77.

122 Cassius Dio, 72.1.1; Herodian 1.3.1; *SHA* 15.5.

123 Gibbon, 1776, I.VII.

124 Hedlund, 2008, 1.1-1.2.

125 Manders, 2012, 13-19.

particularly humiliating blows to the Roman rule: the death in battle of a reigning emperor and his son when Trajan Decius and his son Herennius Etruscus (AD 249-251) died at Abritus in AD 251 in the province of Moesia inferior (the Balkans). This was followed by the capture and death of a reigning emperor when Valerian (AD 253-260) was taken captive by the Sassanid king, Shapur (c. AD 240-272), in the eastern empire. The nature of Roman rule in the third century AD became increasingly military and the period has been categorised as the period of "soldier emperors." [126] In support of this, the portraits of emperors on coins at this time often depicted them in military attire and the reverse inscriptions frequently emphasised the strong relationship between the emperor and the army.[127]

A second identifiable threat in the third century AD was internal instability. While military revolts were not unknown in the earlier imperial period, there are more recorded events of usurpation in this period than at any other time. Between AD 218 and AD 300 fifty-five usurpers can be listed, of whom twenty-five are known to have issued coinage.[128] The distinction between "legitimate" emperors and usurpers was often a very fine line,[129] and the coinage may provide evidence of how legitimation was sought. This book includes a case study of the coinage of the usurper Carausius (AD 286-293) and the extent to which he made use of Golden Age iconography.

A third threat during this period can be labelled dynastic instability. Roman imperial succession had long been seen as a dynastic matter.[130] Augustus had gone to great lengths to present himself as the legitimate heir of Julius Caesar and ensured that power was inherited by members of the imperial family.[131] Septimius Severus made extensive claims in presenting himself as successor to the Antonines and, in turn, laid emphasis on future dynastic stability through his sons.[132] The support of the army, however, became a vital new factor in this period. During the third century, therefore, dynastic succession was more strongly linked with other claims. It has been said that: "increasingly, those who became emperors with the support of the army found it expedient to resort to other forms of legitimation of a sacred or religious nature." [133] This book aims to examine the numismatic evidence for links between Golden Age iconography, the Saecular Games and claims of dynastic continuity.

126 De Blois, 2002, 206; Hedlund, 2008, 94.
127 Watson, 1999, 171; the term "military anarchy" was used to label this period: Rostovtzeff, 1926.
128 Casey, 1994, 35-36.
129 Watson, 1999, 5.
130 Hekster, 2015, 2.
131 Kemezis, 2014, 120-126.
132 See Chapter 2.1.
133 Lo Cascio, 2005, 157.

Other issues faced by the Roman Empire at this time included major economic problems [134] and, what has been labelled a "spiritual crisis." [135] While there are comparatively few surviving military and political records from the period, the third century AD saw a huge outpouring of writings of a spiritual or philosophical nature.[136] New intellectual developments coincided with a renewal of interest in Greek thought, in a trend that has been called the Second Sophistic.[137] Neoplatonism has been described as "one of the greatest cultural achievements of the third century." [138] This religious philosophy, based on the ideas of Plato, developed in Egypt under the influence of Plotinus.[139] Along with other philosophies of the time, Neoplatonism engaged in narratives of cyclical decline and renewal. [140]

The same period saw a great increase in writings on Christianity which often took as their discussion point what has been termed the "political theology of the Augustan revolution".[141] These Christian writings frequently discuss eschatological ideas which also incorporate decline and renewal concepts.[142] Christianity did not emerge from a vacuum, and its doctrines and norms developed in close engagement with Graeco-Roman culture.[143]

The third century also saw the continued growth of so-called mystery cults such as those of Cybele, Isis and Mithras.[144] While little information on these cults survives, the themes of renewal, rebirth and eternity seem to have been incorporated into their beliefs.[145] An apparent characteristic of Roman religious culture at this time was so-called syncretism.[146] The classic exposition of this is the famous prayer to Isis in Apuleius's *Metamorphoses,* in which Isis appears to be identified with ten other female goddesses.[147] This syncretic approach can also be seen, perhaps, in the different names given to Lucina

---

134 2012, Estiot, 539-545; De Blois, 2002, 215; Watson, 1999, 11.

135 Hedlund, 2008, 5; Dodds 1965.

136 Ando, 2012, 122.

137 Goldhill,2001; Urbano, 2014, 49.

138 Watson, 1999, 16.

139 Ousager, 2004.

140 Urbano, 2014, 45; Holliday, 1990, 542-3.

141 Brent, 2009, 78-128.

142 Brent, 2010, 96-116 on St Cyprian's dialogue with pagan culture.

143 Van Nuffelen, 2011, 217.

144 Turcan, 1996; the coinage of the third century displays a much wider range of deities than ever before – see Manders (2012) 96 and Steyn, 2013, 31.

145 Dowling, 2004, 184; Liebeschuetz, 1979, 221.

146 Forsyth,2012, 133; Beard, North Price, 1998, 2.9. See Plutarch, *Moralia*, 67 for a straightforward rationale.

147 Apuleius, Metamorphoses, XI 5; see also Nonnus, *Dionysiaca*, XI.392-410; but see Martin, 2005, 286-294 on the complexities of syncretism.

in the *Carmen Saeculare*.[148] In reviving the Saecular Games, Augustus and his advisers gave the impression of a traditional religious revival.[149] So, for example, Greek rites[150] and the names of Greek deities were included in the rituals. Even Horace's *Carmen Saeculare* is in the form of an ancient Greek paean.[151] One explanation seems to be that the Greek elements of the Saecular Games were part of a syncretic approach which "lent an aura of antiquity," [152] although much of the ritual was essentially Roman.[153] Nonetheless, the inclusion of the Greek rites may have served to flatter a philhellenic section of Roman aristocracy,[154] and may also have served to highlight the presence of foreign practices at Rome in order to legitimate Roman imperialism.[155]

Pagans and Christians alike were writing, often competitively, about the problems of the third century in eschatological terms of a world reaching collapse before an expected renewal.[156] Cyclical time and a yearning for a return to peace and stability, as with the myth of the Golden Age, were common to many of these discourses.[157]

The key written sources for the third century AD

Although the third century AD is one of least well-documented periods of imperial Roman history, wherever possible, coin iconography is put in the context of contemporary written sources. There are three main writers from the third century AD whose narratives were written in Greek. Perhaps the most important text is that of Cassius Dio whose extensive Roman history was probably written between AD 220-231.[158] Dio held high office in the Severan dynasty and appears to have had first-hand knowledge of the imperial family.[159] Unusually, he writes in a highly anecdotal and personal style. While there has been debate as to whether he was wholly Greek in his outlook more recent opinions tend to see Cassius Dio, in terms of his attitudes, as thoroughly Roman.[160]

---

148   *rite maturos aperire partus lenis, Ilithyia, tuere matres, sive tu Lucina probas vocari seu Genitalis:*
      (O gentle Ilithyia, duly revealing the child at full term, now protect gentle mothers, whether you'd
      rather be known as Lucina or Genitalis). Horace, *Carmen Saeculare*, l.13-16 (translation A. Kline).
149   Lipka (2009)148; Lipka refers to a merger of Greek and Roman rites; Schnegg-Kohler, 2002,118.
150   Beer, 2011; Taylor, 1935, 122-130; Rantala, 2013, 64.
151   Hijmans, 2009, 562.
152   Thomas, 2011, 272.
153   Scheid, 1995, 15-31.
154   Galinsky, 1967, 631; political motives for adopting Greek rites are ascribed by : Poletti, 2018, 551.
155   Scheid, 1995, 30; see Schnegg-Köhler, 2002, for an alternative approach; see Cooley, 2006, 229ff
      for another political aspect of the Saecular games concerning the conquest of Latium.
156   Urbano, 2014, 39-49.
157   Brent, 2010, 149-177.
158   Birley, 1988, 203-204.
159   Rantala, 2013, 25.
160   Rantala, 2013 26.

Secondly there is Herodian, who probably wrote his eight-part history around AD 250. Herodian is usually assessed as a lower-ranking official from a Greek-speaking part of the empire. His writing style is more conservative. He is generally regarded as less factually accurate writer than Dio and when he claims to have been present at particular events, his accuracy is especially doubtful.[161] Nevertheless, Herodian provides history in a reasonably chronological order, from the point of view of an interested contemporary writer.[162] Although he cannot be classified as a historian, the author of 'Apollonius' and the 'Lives of the Sophists', known as Philostratus, is the third of this trio of writers in Greek from the third century.[163]

An interesting written source for the middle of the third century AD sources is the Thirteenth Sybilline Oracle. This contemporary narrative is dressed in an apocalyptic and oracular form but provides an invaluable historical viewpoint from the eastern empire.[164] The writings of Censorinus have already been referenced above and include an important account of the Saecular Games.[165] For the Tetrarchic period, the panegyrics[166] provide key insights into the court rhetoric. These elaborate speeches abound with references that can be linked to the iconography of coinage[167] as has been shown with studies of the Arras hoard.[168]

The later Byzantine accounts probably derive chiefly from the lost third century works of Dexippus. The most important is the work of Zosimus which dates from the sixth century. Zosimus was no supporter of the Christian church and he provides a detailed account of the Saecular Games and its origins. Zonaras, who was writing in the twelfth century, is equally important.[169]

The *Scriptores Historiae Augustae* is also, to some extent, probably based on the works of Dexippus. Parts of the *SHA* are notoriously unreliable. It was adapted through the work of an unknown and unreliable Latin historian, which leaves the work open to much criticism. However, when Dexippus is quoted, the relevant passages may be more trustworthy. [170]

Coins as communication

The debate about the extent to which coins can be seen as vehicles for communication has already been touched on. The coinage examined in this book is mostly very rare and therefore, presumably, was not intended for a wide

161 Kemezis, 2014, 228.

162 Potter, 2004, 232.

163 Kemezis, 2014, 150 -226; Swain, 1991, 148-163.

164 Potter, 1990; Swain, 1992, 375-382.

165 Ovid, Metamorphoses, 1.89-150. O'Mara, 2003, 17-26.

166 Nixon and Rodgers, 1994.

167 Steinbock, 2014, 51- 60; Hedlund, 2008, 5-49.

168 Bastien and Metzger, 1977, 214-216.

169 Banchich and Lane, 2012.

170 Potter, 2004, 233.

circulation. It is a recognised characteristic of governments to engage in the act of self-legitimation. [171] The associated argument, that a relatively small, elite group may have chosen the iconography to reinforce their own legitimation, is a fitting one in this context. In terms of understanding iconography on Roman coinage, it has been pointed out that "symbols are more meaningful to those that wield them than those that passively accept them".[172] In terms of the very rare Augustan coins of the Saecular Games, it has been argued that the meaning of the iconography on the coinage would have been known only to the priests, the priestly college and the magistrates charged with celebrating them on everyone's behalf. In other words, the coinage had extensive significance for a small but elite group of people.[173]

Despite a small circulation, it is argued that the iconography was important in representing the collective political identity of the elite, and their self-legitimation, especially when placed in a context of contemporary rhetoric and art.

This does not mean the symbolism was relevant only to the elite.[174] Some coins minted for the Millennial Saecular Games in AD 248, for example, were issued in much larger numbers. The issue of coin circulation is relevant here. While Roman imperial Coinage (RIC) remains the best reference work for identifying individual coin types, it is not a reliable indicator of coin output or circulation. A more accurate quantitative approach is to examine the numbers of coin types using hoard analysis and site finds to identify the prominence of particular types of coins.[175] Most of coinage featured in this book does not figure in large numbers in known coin hoards; where the exceptions to this occur, hoard analysis has been used to illustrate a wider circulation.

Figure 4: Dupondius of Domitian, Ludi Saeculares sacrifice: (RIC II 621) © CNG image ref: 887640

Domitian's Saecular Games coinage appears to have been produced in greater numbers than those of Augustus.[176] The meaning of the rituals depicted

171 Barker, 2001.

172 Butcher, 2005, 145.

173 Scheid, 1998, 33; Sobocinksi, 2006, 596; given the instability of the third century AD, it was vital to keep supporters close in order to ensure survival.

174 Howgego, 2005, 17.

175 Noreña, 2011, 21- 24; Rowan, 2012, 3-4; but see cautionary note from Bland, 2012, 520.

176 Rowan, 2012, 63 citing quantitive analysis in RIC II.

(e.g. Figure 4, which appears to depict the emperor sacrificing cakes to Ilithyia at the Tarentum) would presumably have been understood by those close to the emperor.[177] For those outside this elite circle the image might have been understood simply at the level that the emperor performed sacrifices at Rome for the benefit of the Roman people.[178]

This book makes frequent reference to medallions of the period. Medallions have been categorised as essentially commemorative or donative and, given the small numbers of surviving examples, they presumably had a restricted circulation.[179] It is highly likely that medallions were given as personal gifts, and their greater size generally provides more space for more detailed images.[180] The distinction between a coin and medallion is sometimes hard to determine and precious metal medallions may have had an equivalent currency value. The iconography of medallions has been included in this book as a vital part of the numismatic record.[181]

It can be argued that the Golden Age imagery of Augustus was intended to have deep significance which was understood by the ruling elite but, at a general level, could also be shared with other citizens. As part of the programme for the legitimation of power, "the Golden Age incorporated a profound faith in Roman regeneration and continuity mingled nonetheless with fears for the destiny of Rome."[182] The writings and inscriptions which recorded the "restored" Augustan religion served as a source of legitimacy for the imperial court and those close to it.[183]

---

177 The reverse image seems to emphasise the ancient Greek aspects of the rituals as it shows the emperor sacrificing with an unveiled head (*capite aperto*) and one of the musicians is playing an *aulos* or double flute, an archaic Greek instrument. Ilythyia or Eileithyia was goddess of childbirth and known as Lucina to the Romans.
178 Sobocinski, 2006, 598.
179 Rowan, 2012, 38.
180 Hedlund, 2008, 48.
181 Toynbee, 1986, 15-16.
182 Holliday, 1990, 544.
183 Macrae, 2016, 142.

2

THE ICONOGRAPHY OF THE SAECULAR GAMES COINAGE OF SEPTIMIUS SEVERUS AND PHILIP I

2.1 The Severan Saecular Games coinage

The written sources

The Golden Age of Augustus can be identified as one of the principal guiding lights for Septimius Severus, the emperor who reigned at the start of the third century (AD 193-211).[184] Like Augustus, Septimius Severus became emperor by triumphing over rivals in civil wars. Didius Julianus, Pescennius Niger and Clodius Albinus and were all defeated and killed in his bloody path to supreme power.[185] It is no wonder that legitimation became such a priority; for example, he was keen to claim descent from the Antonines, amongst others, or as Cassius Dio dryly observes:

> "He caused us especial dismay by constantly styling himself the son of Marcus and the brother of Commodus and by bestowing divine honours upon the latter, whom but recently he had been abusing." [186]

When commenting on the transition from the reign of Marcus Aurelius to Commodus, Dio makes a famous observation which is based on Golden Age myth:

---

184 Barnes, 2008, 257; Cooley, 2007, 391.

185 Eutropius, *Breviarum*, Bk VIII,18.

186 "μάλιστα δ' ἡμᾶς ἐξέπληξεν ὅτι τοῦ τε Μάρκου υἱὸν καὶ τοῦ Κομμόδου ἀδελφὸν ἑαυτὸν ἔλεγε, τῷ τε Κομμόδῳ, ὃν πρῴην ὕβριζεν, ἡρωικὰς." DIO CASSIUS, VOL.IX, translated by Earnest Cary and Herbert B. Foster, Loeb Classical Library Volume 177. Cambridge, Mass,: Harvard University Press, First published 1927. Loeb classical Library ® is registered trademark of the President and Fellows of Harvard.

"This matter must be our next topic, for our history now descends from the kingdom of gold to one of iron and rust, as affairs did for the Romans of that day." [187]

Given that Cassius Dio comments on the association of Septimius Severus with Commodus, this famous remark may be a pessimistic comment on the Severan claim to a Golden Age as well as that of Commodus.

Septimius Severus, who hailed from Leptis Magna in Tripolitania, relied on many of the examples and precedents that Augustus had set in order to secure his position. He wanted to present himself as Augustus had done, as the emperor who restored peace and renewed the empire after the chaos of civil war. [188] One striking action that Septimius Severus took in imitation of Augustus was to renew the Augustan marriage legislation. [189] This was ridiculed by Tertullian:

"Why those absurd Papian laws which require people to have children at an earlier age than the Julian laws require them to be married – did not the valiant emperor Severus clear them out but yesterday for all their old age and authority?" [190]

By renewing these laws, Septimius Severus was following the emphasis that Augustus had put on the moral nature of the new Golden Age. [191]

Herodian's history includes the following passage on the Saecular Games:

"In his reign we saw all kinds of different shows in all the theatres at the same time, including all-night religious ceremonies celebrated in imitation of the Mysteries. These were the ceremonies that were called, at the time, the Saecular Games when people heard that generations had elapsed since they had last been celebrated. Heralds travelled through Rome and Italy summoning all the people to come and attend the Games the like of which they had never seen before and would not see again." [192]

---

187 "περὶ οὗ ἤδη ῥητέον, ἀπὸ χρυσῆς τε βασιλείας ἐς σιδηρᾶν καὶ κατιωμένην τῶν τε πραγμάτων τοῖς τότε Ῥωμαίοις καὶ ἡμῖν νῦν καταπεσούσης τῆς ἱστορίας." DIO CASSIUS, VOL.IX, translated by Earnest Cary and Herbert B. Foster, Loeb Classical Library Volume 177. Cambridge, Mass,: Harvard University Press, First published 1927. Loeb classical Library ® is registered trademark of the President and Fellows of Harvard.

188 Cooley, 2007, 385-397.

189 Gorrie, 2004, pp 61-72; Cassio Dio, *Historia Romana*, LXXVII.16.

190 "*Nonne vanissimas Papias leges, quae ante liberos suscipi cogunt quam Iuliae matrimonium contrahi, post tantae auctoritatis senectutem heri Severus, constantissimus princeps exclusit.*" Tertullian, *Apologia*, 4.8 (translation by T Glover).

191 Galinsky, 1996, 96.

192 HERODIAN, VOL.1, translated by C.R.Whittaker, Loeb Classical Library Volume 454, Cambridge, Mass,: Harvard University Press, Copyright © 1969 by the President and Fellows of Harvard College. Loeb Classical Library ® is a registered trademark of the President and Fellows of Harvard College.

The *SHA* contains no mention of the Saecular Games. The later rewriting of the histories tended to focus on the first five or six years of the rule of Septimius Severus. They abandon any attempt at detailed narrative for the later part of the reign,[193] either because they did not see it as important or, possibly, they wanted to prioritise more dramatic pieces of history.[194]

Dio's surviving account of Septimius Severus's reign appears to leave out explicit reference to the Saecular Games. It had been assumed that later errors in copying of Dio's work conflated the *Decennalia* celebrations of AD 202 and the *Ludi Saeculares*. It has also been suggested that this may have been a deliberate omission by Dio in order to highlight the extravagance of Septimius Severus[195] and provide a better narrative for the fall of Plautianus.[196] Further, this account may indicate that Dio could not bring himself to describe the Saecular Games as he felt they falsely represented the success of the Severan dynasty.[197] Whatever the reason, there is a striking similarity between a list of animals in Dio's account and the list of animals in the surviving Severan *commentarii* of AD 204. The passage in Dio runs as follows:

> *"The entire receptacle in the amphitheatre had been constructed so as to resemble a boat in shape, and was capable of receiving or discharging four hundred beasts at once; and then as it suddenly fell apart, there came rushing forth bears, lionesses, panthers, lions, ostriches, wild asses, bison (this is a kind of cattle foreign in species and appearance) so that seven hundred beasts in all, both wild and domesticated, at one and the same time were seen running about and were slaughtered."[198]*

The Severan *commentarii*, inscribed on the monumental marble *cippus*, includes this sentence: *"Through our munificence there were a hundred each of lions, lionesses, leopards, bears, bison, wild asses, ostriches."* [199]

It may be significant that seven types of animals are mentioned here and that the total number of beasts is given as seven hundred. The Severan

---

193 Birley,1988, 160.

194 Rantala, 2013, 29.

195 Rowan, 2012,52; Carlson, 1969, 20-1.

196 Scott, 2017,158.

197 Scott, 2017, 160.

198 "τῆς δὲ δεξαμενῆς ἀπάσης τῆς ἐν τῷ θεάτρῳ ἐς πλοίου σχῆμα κατασκευασθείσης ὡς τετρακόσια θηρία καὶ δέξασθαι καὶ ἀφεῖναι ἀθρόως, ἔπειτα ἐξαίφνης διαλυθείσης ἀνέθορον ἄρκτοι λέαιναι πάνθηρες λέοντες στρουθοὶ ὄναγροι βίσωνες 'βοῶν τι τοῦτο εἶδος, βαρβαρικὸν τὸ γένος καὶ τὴν ὄψιν', ὥστε ἑπτακόσια τὰ πάντα καὶ θηρία καὶ βοτὰ ὁμοῦ καὶ διαθέοντα ὀφθῆναι καὶ σφαγῆναι." DIO CASSIUS, VOL.IX, translated by Earnest Cary and Herbert B. Foster, Loeb Classical Library Volume 177. Cambridge, Mass,: Harvard University Press, First published 1927. Loeb classical Library® is registered trademark of the President and Fellows of Harvard College.

199 *Munificen[tia] nostra leones lea[e] leopardi ursi bisones onagri str[uthiones] centeni erunt*; Pighi, 1941, 161, 43.

commentarii declare the Saecular Games to be the seventh celebration, [200] whereas Censorinus refers to them as the eighth in the series.[201] It may be that Septimius Severus was obsessed with the number seven,[202] partly because of the reference in his own name, Septimius, partly because the number was of significance in the birth and growth of children, [203] and partly because of the seven planets in Roman astrology.

As discussed above, astrology was key to the myth of the Augustan Golden Age and Cassius Dio notes Septimius Severus's keen interest in astrology.[204] There is even a claim that, before becoming emperor, Septimius Severus was indicted and acquitted for consulting astrologers. [205]

The Severan Building Programme

The emperor's building programme in Rome was the most ambitious since the time of Augustus.[206] Septimius Severus emulated Augustus by winning a victory against Parthia when he captured Ctesiphon.[207] The location of the triumphal arch, built in the forum at Rome in AD 203 to commemorate the Parthian victory, had great symbolic significance: it was placed diagonally opposite the arch of Augustus which commemorated a Parthian victory over two hundred years earlier; thus emphasising a natural cycle of renewal.[208] The restoration of the Porticus Octaviae, which was adjacent to major sites in the Saecular Games, emphasised his renewal of the City and associated himself with Augustus and Alexander the Great.[209]

One of the the grandest new buildings to be seen in Rome was a colossal decastyle temple to Hercules and Dionysus – the emperor's patron gods – on the Quirinal Hill; this is thought to have been the largest temple in the Roman Empire at that time.[210] Part of the reason for this programme of new building and restoration was Septimius Severus's need to legitimise his claim to the throne and indeed many new and restored buildings were related to events at the Saecular Games. [211]

---

200 Pighi, 1941 140. I.1.

201 Censorinus, *De Die Natali*, XVII, 18.

202 See reference to the Septizodium below; Rantala, 2013,130.

203 Rantala, 2013, 125. Censorinus, *De Die Natali*, XIV,12.

204 Cassius Dio, *Historia Romana*, LXXVII, 11 which claims the emperor had his horoscope painted on his palace ceilings,

205 SHA, Sept. Severus 4.3.

206 Gorrie, 1997, 61-72; Rantala, 2013, 11.

207 *SHA*, Severus, 15 – 16; Herodian, History, 3.9; Birley, 1988, 129 – 145.

208 Gorrie, 2007,4; Kemezis, 2014, 68.

209 Gorrie, 2007, 16-17; within the Porticus was a bronze statue depicting Alexander's victory at Granicus.

210 Carandini, 2017, 2 Tab 194.

211 Gorrie, 2002, 461-481.

The main record of the Saecular Games of AD 204, though fragmentmentary, is the inscription (*commentarii*) set up on Campus Martius – the same location where Augustus set up his record of the games. The inscription preserved the *memoria* (memory) of the games.[212]

Figure 5: Severan Ludi Saeculares Commentarii fragment - Museo Nazionale Romano photo by G Barker. Juno Regina appears in the second line.

One of the many new monuments erected by Septimius Severus in Rome was the Septizodium which dominated an area at the foot of the Palatine Hill and may have had representations of the seven planetary deities reflecting emperor's place in, and control over, the cosmos.[213]

Severan Patron Deities

Hercules and Bacchus were the tutelary deities of Septimius's native city, Leptis Magna, (Figure 6) but came to have great significance over the whole reign of Septimius Severus.[214] Given the extent to which Commodus was adopted as his model, it is possible that the inclusion of Hercules was another way in which Septimius Severus emulated his adopted brother.[215]

The choice of the two gods Hercules and Bacchus may have other Augustan reference points. Hercules had become a god through the very Roman quality of *virtus*[216] which had been emphasised by Horace as a key quality of the new Augustan Golden Age. It should also be noted that the temple of Hercules Victor is mentioned as one of the venues for preparatory ceremonies in the Augustan *Commentarii*.[217]

---

212 CIL 6.32326-25; Elsner, 1996, 52; Cooley, 2009, 2.

213 Gorrie, 1997, 193.

214 Howgego, 2005, 3; Cooley, 2007, 392; the presiding deity for Domitian was probably Minerva - see Rowan, 2012, 41-45.

215 Rowan, 2012, 47-48; see Medallion of Septimius Severus as Hercules: Gnecchi 1912 (111) 39 no 1.

216 Gersht, 2013, 201.

217 Augustus, *Commentarii Ludi Saeculares,* CIL VI 32323.

Figure 6: Hercules sculpture from the Basilica at Leptis Magna © Image from Featurepics

The link to an Augustan precedent can also be seen in Virgil's *Aeneid*. In the key prophetic passage, when Aeneas is told that Augustus will restore the Golden Age (see Introduction), Augustus is compared to two conquering gods, Hercules and Bacchus.

> *Hercules, in truth, never crossed as much of the earth's territory, though he brought down the bronze-footed Arcadian deer, pacified and protected the woods of Erymanthus, made Lerna quake at his bow: Nor triumphant Bacchus, who drives his chariot with reins made of vines, guiding his tigers down from Nysa's high peak.²¹⁸*

The implication here is that Augustus will exceed the greatness of Hercules and Bacchus as later stated explicitly by Tacitus when listing those mortals who became gods:

> *And so Hercules and Bacchus among the Greeks and Quirinus among us were enrolled in the number of the gods. Augustus, did better, seeing that he had aspired.²¹⁹*

The choice of these particular comparators carries another key meaning. Virgil is also likening Augustus to the conqueror Alexander the Great as panegyrics and encomia of the period often linked Alexander the Great to these gods.²²⁰ For example, the same comparison, linking Augustus to these gods, and therefore Alexander, can be found in the Odes of Horace. ²²¹

---

218 Virgil, *Aeneid* VI, 801-805: *nec vero Alcides tantum telluris obivit, fixerit aeripedem cervam licet, aut Erymanthi pacarit nemora et Lernam tremefecerit arcu; nec qui pampineis victor iuga flectit habenis Liber, agens celso Nysae de vertice tigris (translation G Barker).*

219 Tacitus, *Annales* 4.37-38: *sic Herculem et Liberum apud Graecos, Quirinum apud nos deum numero additos: melius Augustum, qui speraverit (translation by A J Church and W J Brodribb).*

220 Reed, 1998, 413; nie ewski, 2007, 108.

221 Horace, *Odes*, 3.3. Statius explicitly links the two gods with Alexander: Statius, *Silvae*, 6.

Alexander the Great claimed descent from Herakles (Hercules in the Roman pantheon) who, like Alexander, was a son of Zeus. Mythical accounts of his birth involved references to thunderbolts (representing Zeus), the seal of a lion (representing Herakles) and a snake (representing Dionysus or Bacchus in the Roman pantheon). [222]

It is thought that Hercules and Liber Pater may also have acted as guardian deities of the two princes, Caracalla and Geta.[223] This would link the two gods with the continuity of a new Golden Age and a new dynasty.[224]

The Severan Coinage

The Saecular Games coinage of Septimius Severus is rare and would have had a limited circulation, as discussed in the introduction. One such rare coin (Figure 7) is an *aureus* from the mint at Rome which features gods associated with these games. Hercules stands on the right holding his club and lion-skin and Liber Pater (Dionysus) stands left, holding cup and thyrsus, with a small panther visible to the lower left.

Figure 7: Aureus of Septimius Severus (RIC IV 257) © British Museum: 1909,0505.13

This was the first time these deities appeared together on Roman imperial coinage and perhaps indicates the importance of these gods to Septimius Severus, not only as his *di patrii* (native gods) but also as his *dis auspicibus* (auspicious gods), and proclaims their influence over the new Golden Age of Septimius Severus. The same design appeared on a *denarius* which is equally rare.

The reverse inscription on this *aureus* dates the issue to the emperor's third consulship (COS III), AD 204, and declares when the Saecular Games were held. Septimius Severus appears to have followed the precise formula set by Horace in the *Carmen Saeculare*[225] and in the *Res Gestae* for Augustus.[226] Accordingly, Severus celebrated his Games AD 204, exactly 220 years, or two *saecula* of 110 years each, after the Saecular Games of Augustus in 17

---

222 Herodotus, Histories, VIII; Plutarch, Life of Alexander, 2-3.

223 Rantala, 2016, 73.

224 Fears, 1981, 114-115.

225 Horace, *Carmen Saeculare*, l.21. See Appendix II.

226 *Res Gestae Divi Augustus*, 22.2.

BC.[227] Saecular Games coins with the two deities were also issued in the name of Caracalla (Figure 8), and hoard analysis reveals they were not struck in any great quantity, with only five known examples in the name of Septimius Severus[228] and four known examples of Caracalla's[229] issue.[230]

Figure 8: Denarius of Caracalla (RIC IV 74a) © British Museum: 1907,1007.12

Septimius Severus followed the Augustan precedent of issuing coins with a dated *cippus*, which may have formed part of the record of the occasion, as discussed in the introduction. A novel aspect of the reverse design is the inclusion of the patron gods on either side of *cippus* (Figure 9). The same design appears on equally rare coins of Caracalla (Figure 10).

Figure 9: As of Septimius Severus (RIC IV 764A) © American Numismatic Society: 1951.94.24

227 Fears, 1981, 114-115.
228 RIC IV 257.
229 RIC IV 74a.
230 Rowan, 2012, 58.

Figure 10: As of Caracalla (RIC IV 420) © CNG image Triton Auction 1, Lot 1551, December 1997

A remarkable piece of iconography is depicted on a *sestertius* issued by the Rome mint (Figure 11).[231] The reverse design appears to be similar to the bronze Saecular Games coinage of Domitian (see example at Figure 4). The emperor is sacrificing, standing left. Also shown is a double-flute player (centre) and a *victimarius* with pig (lower right). The extraordinary feature of the design is the inclusion of the patron gods, Hercules and Liber Pater, standing right. [232] Caracalla also issued coins with this design (see Figure 167).[233]

Figure 11: Sestertius of Septimius Severus (RIC IV 761) © The Fitzwilliam Museum, Cambridge

While the dated *cippus* design and the LVDOS SAECVL FEC followed examples from Augustus and Domitian, Septimius Severus also issued a novel reverse inscription to celebrate the Saecular Games. These were the rare issues with the legend SACRA SAECVLARIA (Figures 12-14).

231 Rantala, 2016, 73; Cooley, 2007, 392.

232 The reclining figure of Tellus, identified by the sacrificial pig, is discussed in Chapter 5.1.

233 See also coin in Hunterian collection: GLAHM:28598.

Figure 12: Sestertius of Septimius Severus (RIC IV 816a) © British Museum: 1872,0709.772   1

The reverse depicts three veiled figures, probably the emperor with his two sons, sacrificing over an altar in front of a canopy. Two musicians stand either side – a harpist and a flute player – and the reclining figure to the left probably represents the river Tiber. The scene almost certainly depicts one of the sacrifices at the Saecular Games in Rome. The background is probably the temporary wooden theatre, mentioned in the *commentarii* which record the Severan Saecular Games.[234] Although the reverse inscription is novel, the design is reminiscent of the coinage of Domitian, who issued a whole series of coins depicting rituals from the Saecular Games (e.g. see Figure 4). Domitian's coins show the emperor sacrificing with head uncovered as in the Greek rite. The Severan coins show the emperor sacrificing with a veiled head (i.e. in the Roman fashion). While the rituals appeared to reflect ancient Greek ritual,[235] in fact, they seem to have been thoroughly Roman, as discussed in the introduction.[236] Other coins issued by Septimius Severus and Geta from the Rome mint depict two veiled figures facing each other as they sacrifice and a *denarius* with a similar reverse (Figures 13 and 14).

Figure 13: As of Geta (RIC IV 132) © CNG e-auction 280, Lot 233 June 2012

---

234 Pighi, 1941, 161. line V.44; Hill, 1964, 175.

235 The *commentarii* refer to "*Archivo Graeco Ritu*" (ancient Greek ritual); Pighi, 1941, 156, line IV.6.

236 Scheid, 1995, 15-31.

The coinage with TRP XII or COS III for Septimius Severus, described above, can be firmly dated to AD 204 but the dating of the SACRA SAECVLARIA coinage is not straightforward. These coins may have been commemorative issues.[237] They emphasise the involvement of the princes in the Saecular Games rituals, as recorded in the *commentarii*.[238] The continued use of this reverse inscription, unique to the Severan period, appears to celebrate the reign of this dynasty as a sacred age.[239]

Figure 14: Denarius of Septimius Severus (RIC IV 293a) © Wildwinds

Coinage with the reverse inscription SAECVLI FELICITAS issued by the Severan dynasty is mainly covered in Chapter 4, though some examples are illustrated in this section where they relate directly to the Saecular Games. A Severan coin issue (Figure 15) which is similar to coins issued by Augustus (Figure 16)[240] and Domitian[241] is a type usually classified as a *liberalitas* distribution. In fact, the coin more closely resembles the distribution of the *suffimenta*, or materials for purification, which was a ritual performed early in the Saecular Games.[242] The reverse shows the emperor and his two sons on a platform giving *suffimenta* to a citizen on the ground. A priest or official stand behind the urn containing the *suffimenta*. The reverse legend is FELICITAS SAECVLI.

Figure 15: Denarius of Septimius Severus (RIC IV 263) © CNG, Triton sale, January 2003, Lot 937

237 Hill, 1964, 176.
238 Pighi, 1941, 143, I 27-28.
239 Rantala, 2013, 85.
240 It has been noted that this coin, minted by Mescinius Rufus, is among the first coins to represent living people in action: Morrell, Osgood & Welch, eds, 2019,211.
241 RIC II, 600-605.
242 Rowan, 2012, 61.

A similar design was issued in bronze coinage in the names of Caracalla[243] and Geta[244] who are recorded as having taken part in the Saecular Games rituals.[245]

Figure 16: Aureus of Augustus © CNG Auction, Triton 5, January 2002, Lot 1857

Another issue in Caracalla's name (Figure 17), with the reverse inscription FELICITAS SAECVLI may show the *fruges* ceremony where citizens brought gifts of agricultural produce as depicted on coins of Domitian (Figure 18).[246]

Figure 17: As of Caracalla (RIC IV 470) © British Museum: R.15803

The Severan coinage also emphasised the new dynasty, such as this *aureus* of Caracalla (Figure 19) which features his parents on the reverse under the inscription CONCORDIAE AETERNAE (eternal concord). The emperor and his consort are portrayed as the sun and moon (he with the radiate crown and she with a crescent moon). As such, they represent a "cosmic couple" of a new Golden Age who will bring stability and continuity to the empire.[247] Again, there may be a link to Apollo and Diana, who feature in the Severan *Carmen Saeculare* as well as in the rituals themselves.[248] Further, the image may also illustrate the link between the emperor and astrology, mentioned above.

---

243 RIC IV 469.
244 RIC IV 126.
245 Pighi, 1941, 141, I.17.
246 RIC II 1.608; Sobocinski, 2006, 584.
247 Rantala, 2013, 87.
248 Pighi, 1941, 165 & 224; Rantala, 2017, 179.

Figure 18: Sestertius of Domitian (RIC II, 1, 608) © British Museum 1872,0709.508

Figure 19: Aureus of Caracalla (RIC IV 52) © British Museum: 1844,0425.2315

The image of *Roma Aeterna* and her temple was to appear with increasing frequency in the third century, starting with Septimius Severus.[249] The idea of *imperium sine fine* (empire without end)[250] had been established in the reign of Augustus under whom the concept was embodied by the presence of the emperor.[251] From the time of Trajan's reign, *aeternitas* became particularly associated with *imperium* and was a key aspect of the *saeculum aureum*.[252] The emperor Hadrian (AD 117-138), as a "second Augustus" [253] used Golden Age symbolism extensively (see Figure 117) and created the cult of *Urbs Roma Aeterna*.[254] When he instituted the *Natalis Urbis Romae Aeternae* (on April 21st), Hadrian was continuing and extending Augustan policy.[255] The image of the seated goddess Roma became a familiar coin type from the time of Hadrian [256] as part of the iconography associated with a new Golden Age.[257] At Figure 20, Roma holds images of the sun and moon in her hand, emphasising the

---

249 Boatwright, 1987, 119-133.

250 Virgil, *Aeneid*, 1. 279.

251 MacCormack, 1981, 62.

252 Versnel, 1993, 202.

253 Toynbee, 1986, 140; Abdy, 2019, 39.

254 Fishwick, 2002, 192.

255 Boatwright, 1987, 119-133.

256 Melville Jones, 1990, 272.

257 Walton, 1957, 167; e.g. RIC II 263a.

cosmological aspect to the eternity of Rome, and may be linked to the Augustan Golden Age of Apollo and Diana. It has been pointed out that the year AD 124 marked 110 years, or an Augustan *saeculum*, since the deification of Augustus and this, in itself, may have led to the renewed Gold Age imagery.[258]

The *Romae Aeternae* coinage of Septimius Severus is very rare, and the image on an *aureus* (Figure 21) follows the design of the Hadrianic coinage with Roma holding the Palladium, though coins were also issued showing Roma holding a victory figure, instead of the Palladium. Equally rare is the coinage with the same reverse which was issued in the name of Caracalla, Geta, and Julia Domna.[259] Alexander Severus, would later issue a series of coins with this reverse.[260]

Figure 20: Aureus of Hadrian (RIC II 263) © British Museum: R.12136

Figure 21: Aureus of Septimius Severus (RIC IV 291) © CNG auction Triton VI, Lot 934, January 2003

The Severan *commentarii* highlight Julia Domna's role as wife and mother.[261] Rare coinage was issued in Julia Domna's name with the reverse Juno Lucinae when she was probably past child-bearing age; so this is probably not a reference to her fecundity (Figure 22).[262] The goddess Lucina who was seen a protector of childbirth was associated with both Juno and Diana. Lucina features in Virgil's *Eclogue*, in the *Carmen Saeculare*[263] and in the Severan

258 Abdy, 2019,40.
259 RIC IV 134a, RIC IV 19, RIC IV 613.
260 RIC IV 175, 602-607.
261 Pighi, 1941, 149, III.9.
262 Sowers, 1995,133.
263 Horace, Carmen Saeculare, l.15; see Appendix II.

Saecular Games inscription[264] so, as well as emphasising the maternal role of the empress,[265] Julia Domna is associated with the birth of a new Golden Age.[266] Further examples of Julia Domna's coinage are discussed in Chapter 5.1.

Figure 22: Sestertius of Julia Domna (RIC IV 857) © CNG Auction 100, Lot 1926, October 2015

As discussed above, the passage from Dio which contains a description of a boat structure and a list of animals at a spectacular celebration, is likely to be describing part of the Saecular Games.[267] There are coins issued by Septimius Severus and by Caracalla which seem to illustrate this event, such as this *aureus* of Septimius Severus with the reverse inscription LAETITIA TEMPORVM - the joyfulness of the times (Figure 23). In the centre is a ship with a sail round which are four racing *quadrigae* and seven animals which appear to include an ostrich, a lion, a tiger, a leopard and a bison. The close correlation with the list of animals both in the *commentarii* and in Dio has been well documented.

Figure 23: Aureus *of Septimius Severus (RIC IV 274) © Roma Numismatics Auction 4, Lot 574, September 2012 https://www.romanumismatics.com*

264 Pighi, 1941, 141, l. 18; Rantala 2013, 76.

265 Hekster, 2015, 147.

266 Rantala, 2011, 157-172.

267 Rowan, 2012, 51-52.

The coin is not dated but is categorised in RIC with Rome mint issues between AD 202-210. This series includes specific Saecular Games coinage such as the *aureus* at Figure 7. The same image and inscription appear on the coinage of Caracalla (Figure 24) and Geta.[268] This repetition may highlight Caracalla as the heir apparent and his part in providing such a spectacular part of the Saecular Games.

Figure 24: Denarius of Caracalla (RIC IV 157) © *CNG Auction, Nomos 2, Lot 199, May 2010*

The same design appears on an intaglio, probably of the same date, where the image on the coin has been reversed (Figure 25). If used as seal, then the image would appear the same as on the coin design.

Figure 25: Intaglio of ship, quadrigae and seven animals © *Martin-von-Wagner-Museum der Universität Würzburg; photo by Christina Keifer*

This intaglio, from the Martin-von-Wagner Museum in Würzburg, shows four *quadrigae* and seven animals including an ostrich which, this time, appears on the right side. The intaglio suggests a close link between the production of coins and gems as well as the involvement of the emperor and his court.[269] It may also suggest that image would be recognised as imperial iconography across the empire.[270]

268 RIC IV 43.
269 Marsden, 2011, 427-434; Henig, 1986, 378-379.
270 Rowan, 2012, 67.

A rare dated *aureus* of Septimius Severus with a reverse inscription SAECVLI FELICITAS may also depict an important aspect of the Severan Saecular Games (Figure 26). A central female figure, usually described as Felicitas, though she may represent Tellus, holds a cornucopia and a basket of fruits.

Figure 26: Aureus of Septimius Severus (RIC IV 327) © Vienna Kunsthistorisches Museum: RÖ 1446

The RIC description records two small figures to her right and three figures to her left. In fact, there are three figures on either side and these could be representations of the children who sang the *Carmen Saeculare* which was specially commissioned for the Severan Games.[271] The performance of this work by the chorus of children on the last day of the Saecular Games probably represented "the continuity and the beginning of a new youthful Golden Age for the empire." [272] The Augustan and the Severan inscriptions record 27 boys and 27 girls, the number 27 being derived from the sacred number three [273] (3x3x3). The Severan inscription records the names of the boys and girls who are described as *pueri senatores* and *puellae matronae,* that is to say children of the senatorial and highest rank.[274] If this interpretation is correct, it may support the idea, outlined in the introduction, that the limited issues of the Saecular Games coinage were mainly intended for circulation amongst those who participated in the rituals and ceremonies. The recipients may have included the children who performed the *Carmen Saeculare.*[275]

Summary

Septimius Severus went out of his way to emulate Augustus by celebrating the Saecular Games in AD 204 in order to usher in a new Golden Age. He

271 Such fragments that survive are recorded in Pighi, 1941, 221-228.

272 Rantala, 2013, 154.

273 Virgil, *Eclogues* VIII, 75. *"numero deus impare gaudet"* (an uneven number pleases the gods) Translation by G Barker. The number three is emphasised in the *Carmen Saeculare,* line 23: see appendix II; the number 27 has many sacred connotations and can be seen as a key number in the so-called Platonic Lambda: Plato, *Timaeus,* 35b.

274 Pighi, 1941,169, VII, l 84-90.

275 Cf. the *sestertius* of Domitian, inscribed COX XIIII LVD SAEC FEC, showing the emperor with three children RIC II 1. 616.

followed the formula, prescribed in the Augustan literature and inscriptions, by celebrating the games 220 years, or two *saecula*, after the Augustan games in 17 BC. Many of his preparatory actions for the games followed an Augustan pattern, including his building programme in Rome. The inscription which recorded the games *(commentarii)* was set up, like that of Augustus, on the Campus Martius.

A striking sentence from the *commentarii* may be reconstructed as follows:

"For the security and eternity of empire you should attend, with all due worship and veneration of the immortal gods, the most holy shrines for the offering and giving of thanks in order that the immortal gods may pass on to future generations all that our ancestors have set up." [276]

This quotation appears to sum up the hopes of the revived Golden Age that Septimius Severus went to such lengths to bring about. The public worship and veneration of the gods by the emperor is strongly illustrated on Severan coinage, especially on the coins with the novel inscription SACRA SAECVLARIA. Even though the coinage is rare, a message which could be understood at a general level was imperial piety for the benefit of the empire.[277] It could also be understood that security was established by a new dynasty. Coins which showed the imperial family, with reverse inscriptions such as CONCORDIAE AETERNAE (Figure 19), ROMA AETERNA (Figure 21) and SAECVLI FELICITAS (see ahead Figure 77), underscored the eternity of a new age for future generations.

Following a protracted civil war, one of the key driving forces for Septimius Severus was the need to legitimise his rule. The full meaning of the rituals, illustrated by the limited issues of Saecular Games coinage, would only have been understood by an initiated elite.[278] This probably reflects the importance of legitimation, as discussed above. The sacred rituals were followed by magnificent games, races and displays, which are shown on certain coins (Figures 23 and 24) and which are described in the *commentarii*.[279] The Saecular Games coinage of Septimius Severus is rare, and more detailed images were intended for initial distribution to an inner circle; though all coinage would have entered a more general circulation in a moneyed section of society.[280] While the rituals, illustrated on the coinage, ushered in a new bountiful Golden

---

276 *Omnique cultu adque veneratione immortalium [....]pro securitate adque aeternitate imperii sanctissimoque locos agendis habendisque gratis frequentetis, ut posteris dii immortales referant, quae maiores nostris condiderunt quaeque ante maioribus ea contulerint, etiam temporibus nostris concesserunt.* Pighi, 1941, 142. 1.23-24 (translation G Barker); Lane Fox, 1986, 464; see also Ando, 2012, 125-126.

277 Scheid, 1998, 30-31.

278 Scheid, 1998, 32; Scheid also considers that deliberate 'errors' on the coinage may have encrypted the precise meaning of the rites: 1998, 32.

279 Pighi, 1941, 161, V 38-48.

280 Rowan, 2012, 77.

Age, the combination of ritual and spectacle "was, for the emperor, a chance to manifest his power and legitimise his rule".[281]

2.2 The Millennial Saecular Games coinage of Philip I

The written sources

In some ways, the reign of Philip I is typical of Roman Imperial rulers of the mid third century AD. Provincially born, in Roman Syria, Philip I became emperor while serving as Praetorian Prefect on the front line of the eastern empire.[282] He was declared emperor by the army in March AD 244, following the sudden death of his predecessor, Gordian III. Five years later he was to die in battle against Decius, the man who would succeed him.

There are aspects of Philip's reign that are uncertain because the ancient sources contain conflicting accounts. Philip is accused by some writers of being responsible for the death of Gordian III, but this is by no means certain.[283] Furthermore, later Christian writers claim that Philip was a Christian, though this seems unlikely based on the evidence available. [284]

What is beyond doubt is that Philip celebrated the Saecular Games in AD 248, which set his reign apart in a very special way. This was to be last officially recorded celebration of these sacred Games. The written sources and the coinage make clear that these were no ordinary celebrations, as they marked the millennium of the foundation of Rome. Ancient written references to the Saecular Games include a comment from Eutropius (4th century AD):

> "In their reign the thousandth year of the city of Rome was celebrated with games and spectacles of vast magnificence." [285]

A little more detail is included in the Chronicles of Cassiodorus (6th century AD). The reference here to the three days and nights appears to refer to the Saecular Games ceremonies such as those recorded by Augustus and Septimius Severus:

> "Under the Consuls Aemilianus and Aquilinus the thousandth anniversary of the city of Rome was celebrated, and with due solemnity Philip and his son arranged the slaughter of innumerable beasts in the great circus. Theatrical spectacles were put on in the Campus Martius

---

281 Rantala, 2013,19.

282   Southern, 2001, 91.

283 Pohlsander,1980, 464.

284 Brent, 2010, 129.

285 *"His imperantibus millesimus annus Romae urbis ingenti ludorum apparatu spectaculorumque celebratus est."* Eutropius, *Breviarium,* 4th century AD, Liber IX. 3 (translation by Revd J S Watson 1853).

*and people stayed up to watch rituals being celebrated for three days
and nights."* [286]

Orosius (5ᵗʰ century AD) is one of the later Christian writers to claim that
the Millennial Games were dedicated to Christ:

*"In the third year of his reign he celebrated the thousandth year of
the founding of Rome. This special anniversary was more prestigious
than any previous occasion and the Christian emperor celebrated with
magnificent games. It cannot be doubted that Philip held this sacred
event to honour Christ and the Church, since no writer mentions any
parade on the Capitol nor any sacrificial victims."* [287]

While there is no direct evidence that Philip was Christian, Eusebius,
writing in the fourth century, suggests there could be reason to believe Philip
was a Christian but this is based on a single anecdote.[288] The claim that Philip's
games were dedicated to Christ is probably wishful thinking by later Christian
writers, and is reminiscent of the later attempt by Christian writers to appropriate
Virgil's Fourth *Eclogue* and indeed the whole concept of a Golden Age.[289]

Eusebius records that Origen wrote separate letters to Philip and his wife[290]
but this in itself gives no indication about the imperial family's beliefs. It is
possible there may simply have been a more inclusive approach to the deities of
the time.[291] The Christian writer, Dionysius of Alexandria, in his letter to Fabius
of Antioch, records that Philip's reign was "kinder towards us" but, as has been
pointed out, this does not necessarily prove his Christianity.[292]

Porphyry recorded the fact that Plotinus, the leading neoplatonic
philosopher, arrived in Rome while Philip I was emperor.[293] There is an

---

286 *"Aemilianus and Aquilinus. His conss. millesimus annus urbis Romae expletus est, ob quam
sollemnitatem innumerabiles Philippus cum filio suo bestias in circo magno interfecit ludosque in
campo Martio theatrales tribus diebus ac noctibus populo pervigilante celebravit."* Cassiodorus,
Chronica XXIIII, Philip; (translation G Barker).

287 *"hic primus imperatorum omnium Christianus fuit ac post tertium imperii eius annum millesimus
a conditione Romae annus impletus est. ita magnificis ludis augustissimus omnium praeteritorum
hic natalis annus a Christiano imperatore celebratus est. nec dubium est, quin Philippus huius
tantae deuotionis gratiam et honorem ad Christum et Ecclesiam reportarit, quando uel ascensum
fuisse in Capitolium immolatasque ex more hostias nullus auctor ostendit."* Orosius, *Historiarum
Adversum Paganum Liber* 7, 20 (translation by G Barker).

288 Eusebius, *Historia Ecclesiastica*, VI 34.

289 Lactantius, *Divinae Institutiones*, 1.11, 5.5, 7.2. For a Christian version of the Golden Age see the
last verse of the carol, "It came upon the midnight clear" (Sears 1850).

290 Eusebius, *Historia Ecclesiastica*, VI, 36.

291 De Blois,1978, 41.

292 Pohlsander, 980, 467. See Eusebius, *Historia Ecclesiastica*, VI 41.15.

293 Porphyry, *Vita Plotini*, 3.

assumption by some writers that Plotinus entered Philip's circle[294] but there is no clear evidence of this.

The *SHA* (4th century AD), although suspect as a source generally, may provide intriguing details about the animals that formed part of the spectacle of the Saecular Games:

> *"There were thirty-two elephants at Rome in the time of Gordian (of which he himself had sent twelve and Alexander ten), ten elk, ten tigers, sixty tame lions, thirty tame leopards, ten belbi or hyenas, a thousand pairs of imperial gladiators, six hippopotami, one rhinoceros, ten wild lions, ten giraffes, twenty wild asses, forty wild horses, and various other animals of this nature without number. All of these Philip presented or slew at the Saecular Games. All these animals, wild, tame, and savage, Gordian intended for a Persian triumph; but his official vow proved of no avail, for Philip presented all of them at the saecular games, consisting of both gladiatorial spectacles and races in the Circus, that were celebrated on the thousandth anniversary of the founding of the City, when he and his son were consuls."* [295]

The inclusion of hippopotami and elk is striking and chimes with their representation on the Saecular Games coinage of Philip I and his family (Figures 45-48). This reference and the mention of other historians, such as Dexippus, in this section of the *SHA* may lend greater authenticity to this narrative.[296] It is possible that Gordian III was preparing to celebrate the Saecular Games himself in addition to the Persian Triumph. Whatever Gordian's intention, Philip was able to use the vast menagerie to add spectacle for what must have been the most significant event of his reign.

The contemporary references to Philip's reign in the Thirteenth Sybilline Oracle strongly imply that Rome's survival is at stake and that Rome needs to be kept safe.[297] In commenting on the Millennial Saecular Games, the relevant passage in the Oracle appears to have been written with a view to counteracting the idea that the thousandth anniversary portended some momentous change.

---

294 Zahran, 2001, 97.

295 *"Fuerunt sub Gordiano Romae elephanti triginta et duo, quorum ipse duodecim miserat, Alexander decem, alces decem, tigres decem, leones mansueti sexaginta, leopardi mansueti triginta, belbi, id est hyaenae, decem, gladiatorum fiscalium paria mille, hippopotami sex, rhinoceros unus, argoleontes decem, camelopardali decem, onagri viginti, equi feri quadraginta, et cetera huius modi animalia innumera et diversa; quae omnia Philippus ludis saecularibus vel dedit vel occidit. has autem omnes feras mansuetas et praeterea efferatas parabat ad triumphum Persicum. quod votum publicum nihil valuit. nam omnia haec Philippus exhibuit saecularibus ludis et muneribus atque circensibus, cum millesimum annum in consulatu suo et filii sui celebravit." SHA* 20, 33. (translation by D. Magie).

296 Potter, 2004, 233.

297 Potter, 1990, 212-258; (Oracle lines 21-80).

In fact, the Oracle seeks to provide reassurance about the preservation of Rome by declaring that Rome's rule will be preserved until it has ruled Egypt for 948 years.[298] There are indications of deep religious tensions about the millennial anniversary and the oracle records riots in Alexandria at this time and a pogrom against Christians. [299]

The Oracles of the period generally placed great significance on numbers, and the Thirteenth Sybilline Oracle is no exception. The text makes no clear statement of a particular cycle of renewal e.g. 110 years (*saeculum*) or 540 years (the years between the appearance of the phoenix). It is interesting to note that the writer of the oracle seems not to have chosen a specific cyclical pattern of a set number of years e.g. a saeculom or a Sothic period.[300] This may reflect the fact that, whereas Septimius Severus had celebrated the start of what Censorinus termed a "natural" *saeculum*, Philip was celebrating a "civil" or anniversarial *saeculum*.[301]

Claudius had celebrated the 800th anniversary of Rome with Saecular Games in AD 47.[302] Antoninus Pius is thought to have celebrated the 900th anniversary in AD 147.[303] Philip continued this tradition by celebrating the Saecular games to mark the 1,000[th] anniversary of Rome.

The dated *cippus* coinage of Philip and his family

According to Mattingly and Sydenham, the celebrations for Philip may have been delayed because the emperor was fighting in Dacia. In any case, the coinage issued to mark the Games is identified as having been issued from late in AD 247 and throughout AD 248.[304]

Several issues, in different denominations, depict the classic Saecular Games design of the dated *cippus* with a reverse inscription SAECVLARES AVGG (Figures 27 - 30). As discussed in the introduction, and in context of the Saecular Games of AD 204, the basic design follows an established Augustan pattern indicating, once again, that the striking of the coinage and its initial distribution probably formed part of the ritual itself.[305] These coins record the date that the rituals of the Millennial Saecular Games were carried out in AD 248.

298 Potter,1990, 145.

299 Potter, 1990, 39; (Oracle lines 50-53, 74-78).

300 Potter, 1990, 240.

301 Censorinus, *De Die Natali*, XVII.

302 Tacitus, *Annales*, 11.11; Suetonius, *De Vita Caesarum*, 21.

303 Levick, 2014, 102; Whetstone,1978,25; See Antoninus Pius medallions on the foundation myths of Rome e.g. Gnecchi, 1912, II p 20/97 and some coin issues with Golden age themes e.g. RIC III 309.

304 Mattingly and Sydenham, 1936, 62.

305 Körner, 2002, 257.

Figure 27: Sestertius of Philip I (RIC IV, III, 162) © Vienna Kunsthistorisches Museum: RÖ 18026

For the avoidance of any doubt as to the anniversary of Rome being celebrated, coins were also issued with the dated *cippus* design and a reverse inscription of MILIARIVM SAECVLVM (Figure 28).

Figure 28: Sestertius of Philip I (RIC IV 157a) © British Museum: 1927,0103.18

Philip's Saecular Games coinage reverts to the Augustan and Domitianic style of dated *cippus* coins[306] in that there are no tutelary gods. Septimius Severus, as discussed above, had depicted Liber Pater and Hercules on his Saecular Games coins, including the dated *cippus* issues. Philip's coinage includes issues with the reverse inscription SAECVLVM NOVVM with an image of *Roma Aeterna* (Figure 40), appropriately connecting this goddess with the anniversary celebrations.

---

306 See Figures 1 and 2.

Figure 29: Radiate of Philip I (RIC IV 24c) © Private collection

Following the precedent of Septimius Severus, Philip I issued dated *cippus* coinage in the name of his male heir making clear that his son, Philip II, participated in the sacred rituals. These coins were issued from Rome in several denominations including *Asses* and *Sestertii*, though all are rare issues.[307] The *aureus* from the mint of Rome (Figure 30) has a different consulship indiction number but is dated to the same year as his father. Just two examples are known of this rare coin.[308]

Figure 30: Aureus of Philip II (RIC IV 225) © Vienna Kunsthistoriches Museum: RÖ 70243

Philip also issued *cippus* coinage in the name of his wife Otacilia Severa with the reverse inscription SAECVLARES AVG (Figure 31). As Otacilia could not have held the post of consul there is no consular date but the *cippus* design seems to indicate that she was fully part of the Saecular Games rituals.[309]

---

307 RIC IV 265 a, b, c.
308 Bland, 2014, Cat. 46 a and b.
309 Balbuza, 2014, 194.

Figure 31: As of Otacilia Severa (RIC IV 202b) © British Museum: R39808

The iconography of the Saecular Games on medallions of Phillip I

The medallion at Figure 32 shows the imperial family on the obverse with an inscription of CONCORDIA AUGVSTORVM (the harmony of the Augusti). The reverse shows an image of the imperial family sacrificing in front of a temple with the inscription SAECVLVM NOVVM. Gnecchi records four examples.[310]

Figure 32: Medallion of Philip I (Gnecchi, 1912, II p.99/13) © British Museum: 1872,0709.418

The image of the emperor and his family sacrificing carries an implicit reminder of their *pietas* (piety). With three imperial family portraits on the obverse, the medallions emphasise the importance of a new family dynasty at the beginning of a new *saeculum*. The image on the reverse of this medallion indicates that the rituals set down by Augustus were enacted in order to usher in a new Golden Age. The emperor and his son are shown sacrificing with heads covered. While this is a sign of piety in the Roman rite,[311] also depicted is a musician playing an *aulos* or double flute (as shown on Domitianic and Severan coins) which was an ancient Greek instrument. This may indicate continuation

310 Gnecchi,1912 II, no.13, 99.
311 Cf. the coin of Domitian illustrated at Figure 4.

of the element of "Greek rituals". The Greek element of the Saecular Games, as performed by Augustus, has been discussed in the introduction.

The obverse inscription CONCORDIA AVGVSTORVM (the harmony of the Augusti) is a phrase which appears to have resonance in the Roman concept of cyclical time. As typified by the later writings of Claudian in the fourth century AD, the eternal renewal of time alternated in cycles of *Concordia* and *Discordia*, with good government being represented by *Concordia*.[312]

Figure 33: Medallion of Philip II (Gnechhi, 1912, II p 97/8) © Kunsthistorisches Museum Vienna Ref: RÖ 32241

A medallion with a similar design, (Figure 33) issued in the name of Philip II, may have served to emphasise the continuity of dynasty brought about by the new Golden Age. Gnecchi records four known examples.[313]

Gnecchi also records a medallion with an obverse showing Philip I and Philip II and a reverse inscription SAECVLVM NOVVM. The reverse design is described as being the same as another medallion of Philip I [314] with a dated reverse inscription and a complex design which appears to show a *Liberalitas* ceremony (Figure 34). The medallion illustrated in Gnecchi is very worn and so Cohen's line drawing is reproduced here, though some details may be approximate.

312 Ware, 2012, 117.
313 Gnecchi , 1912, II, no.8, 97; Tav. 108 no.9.
314 Gnecchi, 1912 II, no.8, 98 (which has the same description as no. 6, 94) Tav. 109, no. 3.

Figure 34: Medallion of Philip I (Cohen, 1880, Philip 127 p107) image from Cohen

The scene appears to show two figures, in the middle distance, seated centrally on a platform (probably Philip I and either Otacilia Severa or the figure of *Liberalitas*) flanked by other seated figures, in a large precinct. Behind them is an architectural façade and in the foreground is group of adults and children who cluster round a figure who stands centre left. Both Gnecchi and Toynbee describe the scene as a representation of *Liberalitas*, but the scene may represent citizens bringing agricultural produce as in Figure 18.[315]

The fact that it appears with a reverse inscription SAECVLVM NOVVM indicates its connection with the Saecular Games and the new Golden Age. This, in turn indicates, that Philip I, like Septimius Severus before him, probably carried out the *fruges* ceremony as peformed by Augustus. If this is correct, the background on the medallion may be the enclosure to the Temple of Diana on the Aventine.[316]

A medallion which also features the imperial family on the obverse has a reverse design which, uniquely, shows a scene of the chariot races with *quadrigae* in the Circus Maximus that must have formed part of the Saecular Games (Figure 35). Gnecchi records two known examples.[317]

---

315 Toynbee, 1986, 110-111.

316 One of the four locations for the *fruges* ceremony mentioned in the Augustan *Commentarii* (CIL 32323-4); the venue is also named in the Carmen Saeculare line 69: Appendix II.

317 Gnecchi, 1912 II, no. 12, 99; Tav. 109 no.5.

Figure 35: Medallion of Philip I (Gnecchi, 1912, Vol. II p 99/12) ©Münzkabinett der Staatlichen Museen zu Berlin : 18203431

The inscriptions recording the Augustan and Severan Saecular Games both include clear references to chariot races; [318] the coinage of Septimius Severus alos features chariot races.[319] So, this image is further evidence that Philip celebrated the Saecular Games following the formula set by Augustus.

The SAECVLARES AVGG coinage of Philip I

A new departure in the iconography of Philip's Saecular Games coinage, is the large number of animals depicted on coins with the reverse inscription SAECVLARES AVGG. That these coins were intended for a wider circulation than other Saecular Games coins is indicated by the larger numbers in which they are represented in hoards.

Mattingly and Sydenham identified eight issues under Philip and his family. Coins with reverse SAECVLARES AVGG start appearing in issue V (dated to AD 247/ 248) from the Rome mint with the majority of coins celebrating the new *saeculum* being produced in issue VII/ VIII (AD 248- 249).

The Dorchester hoard contains nearly 7,000 coins of Philip I and his family.[320] Of these, around 7.5 % of coins have reverse inscriptions which contain direct reference to the Saecular Games and the new *saeculum*. The table below shows the frequency of relevant coinage referenced by RIC numbers rather than Cohen numbers as in the original report. Of the 1,001 coins of Otacilia Severa only two had a *saecvlares* or *saecvlvm* reverse inscription. It is interesting to note that, in this hoard, the largest number of relevant coins for Philip I had the dated *cippus* design.

The range of coinage with the reverse inscription "SAECVLARES AVGG" is recorded in RIC. The mint of Rome, for example, issued a series of radiates (*antoniniani*) with this inscription and a range of different animals. While not all of the animals mentioned in the *SHA* are represented on the coinage, it

318 CIL VI.32323 l. 153-4; Pliny, *Historia Naturalis*, VIII 65, Beard, North, Price, 1998, 143.
319 See Figure 23.
320 Mattingly, 1939, 21.

is possible to identify six or seven types of beast including lion (Figure 37), moose or elk, antelope (Figure 39), gazelle, stag and hippopotamus.

Dorchester Hoard			PHILIP I		
RIC	Obverse Name	Reverse type Inscription – design	Total per coin type	Total for Philip I	Total for Hoard
12	Philip I	*Saecvlares Avgg* – lion	62		
15	Philip I	*Saecvlares Avgg* – wolf	56		
20	Philip I	*Saecvlares Avgg* – deer	4		
21	Philip I	*Saecvlares Avgg* – antelope	60		
23	Philip I	*Saecvlares Avgg* – goat (?)	12		
24c	Philip I	*Saecvlares Avgg* – *cippus*	135		
25b	Philip I	*Saecvlvm Novvm* – temple	88		
111	Philip I	*Saecvlares Avgg* – hippo	56		
116b	Otacilia	*Saecvlares Avgg* – hippo	1		
116b var	Otacilia	*Saecvlares Avgg* – hippo	1		
224	Philip II	*Saecvlares Avgg* – goat (?)	62		
Total			537	6,990	20,748

Table I: Dorchester hoard frequency of Saecular Games coins of Philip I

Figure 36: Sestertius of Philip I (RIC IV 159) © CNG auction 84, May 2010, Lot 1272

In addition to the animals that appeared at the Saecular Games, coins were issued with the design of the wolf suckling the legendary twins, Romulus and Remus (Figures 36 and 38). It has rightly been said that, "with the possible exception of the Trojan horse, there is no scene in the whole iconography of classical myth more recognizable than that of the she-wolf and twins".[321] Since the time of Augustus, Romulus and Remus were the special children who heralded the return of the peace of the Golden Age.[322] Augustus made great

321 Wiseman, 1995, viii.
322 Rehak, 2006, 115.

efforts to connect himself and his Golden Age with Romulus in particular[323] and a panel of the Ara Pacis, which probably portrayed the wolf and twins, may have served to identify Augustus with Romulus.[324] Hadrian had made particular use of the image of the wolf and twins on his coinage[325] and now Philip led a glorious revival of this classic piece of iconography at Rome's millennial celebrations to announce his new Golden Age. The RIC listing of coins with the reverse inscription SAECVLARES AVGG runs as follows:

SAECVLARES AVGG – // I	Lion walking right [RIC 12, 13]
SAECVLARES AVGG – // II	She wolf suckling twins [RIC 15, 16]
SAECVLARES AVGG – // III	Gazelle walking left [RIC 17]
SAECVLARES AVGG – // IIII	Antelope walking left [RIC 18]
SAECVLARES AVGG - // V	Stag walking left or right [RIC 19, 20]
SAECVLARES AVGG - // VI	Antelope walking left or right [RIC 21,22]
SAECVLARES AVGG – //	Goat or Elk walking left [RIC 23]

Table II: RIC Philip I SAECVLARES AVGG coins with animal reverses

Figure 37: Radiate of Philip I (RIC IV 12) © Private collection

The mint at Rome seems to have divided into six *officinae*, each of which specialised in a particular animal with *officina* I striking only lions, II she-wolf and lions, III gazelle and elk, IV antelope and hippopotamus, V stag and VI antelopes.

---

323 Virgil, *Aeneid*, I, 291-294; *Aeneid* VIII, 630- 634.
324 Lamp, 2013, 121.
325 E.g. RIC II part 3, 2019, 708 -711.

Figure 38: Figure 3 Radiate of Philip I (RIC IV 15) © Private collection

Figure 39: Radiate of Philip I (RIC IV 21) © Private collection

Coinage with images of *Roma Aeterna*

As already mentioned, the deity that was associated with Philip's Saecular Games is *Roma Aeterna*, whose evolution and association with the Golden Age has been discussed in the previous chapter. Philip issued coins with the reverse inscription ROMAE AETERNAE in his name (Figure 40) and in the name of Otacilia Severa[326] and Philip II. [327]

Figure 40: Aureus of Philip I (RIC IV 25a, p.71) © British Museum: 1896,0608.59

326 RIC IV 140.
327 RIC IV 243, 251.

Confirming the link between *Roma Aeterna* and the new Golden Age, coins were struck with the original inscription SAECVLUM NOVVM and the image of *Roma Aeterna* in her temple (Figure 41). This coin is the only known example, although it is die-linked to a coin of Otacilia Severa.[328]

Figure 41: Aureus of Philip I (RIC IV 25a, p.71) © British Museum:1896,0608.59

The combination of this image and reverse inscription also appears on lower value denominations.[329] All the coinage is rare and in the Beau Street Hoard the radiates (*antoniniani*) with the reverse inscription SAECVLVM NOVVM represent only 1.3% of the coins of Philip I.[330]

Figure 42: Radiate of Philip I (RIC IV 25 b p71) © Private collection

The larger *saecvlvm novum* coinage, such as the *sestertius* at Figure 43, shows an octastyle temple which probably shows the same temple with more detail which the larger space allows. The Rome mint produced the complete range of coinage with this reverse, from *aurei* to radiates (*antoniniani*). The mint at Antioch produced only radiates.

328 Bland, 2014, 106 (Cat.41); RIC IV 118, p.82
329 As: RIC IV 163a; *sestertius*: RIC IV 164; *antoniniani*: RIC IV 25b, RIC 86, RIC 108.
330 Anthony and Abdy eds., 2019.

Figure 43: Sestertius of Philip I (RIC4 164, p.89) © *British Museum: R.3818*

The AETERNITAS AVGG coinage of Philip I

Philip's coinage also included the reverse inscription AETERNITAS AVGG with an image of an elephant with a mahout holding a goad. The elephant is a symbol of imperial might and long life. The rare coins with this image include radiates (*antoniniani*)[331] and *dupondii* (Figure 44).[332] Given that elephants appear in the *SHA* list, these animals may have featured in the Saecular Games and so may provide another symbol of the eternity of the Golden Age celebrated by the rituals.

Figure 44: Dupondius of Philip I (RIC IV 167c) © *British Museum: BNK,R.848*

The SAECVLARES AVGG coinage of OTACILIA SEVERA

Philip's wife, Otacilia Severa, assumed the title of Augusta in AD 244.[333] Her coinage proclaims her role in the imperial family, her fecundity, and the fact that she participated in the Saecular Games (Figure 31). As with her husband and her son, coins were issued which pictured particular animals which probably featured in the Games.

331 RIC IV 58 (Philip I) and RIC IV 246 (Philip II).
332 Melville Jones, 1990, 108.
333 Southern, 2001,92.

Figure 45: Sestertius of Otacilia Severa (RIC IV 264a) © British Museum:
1984,0618

Issued from Rome in AD 248, the *aureus* at Figure 45 is the only known
example.[334] The reverse design also appears on other denominations e.g. RIC
IV 116b. Hippopotami were listed in the *SHA* account, as quoted above, and
were probably some of the major attractions at the Saecular Games.[335]
Another animal to feature on Otacilia's coins was the elk (or moose) which is
also mentioned in the *SHA* list (Figure 46).[336]

Figure 46: Sestertius of Otacilia Severa (RIC IV 264a) © British Museum:
1984,0618

Other coins issued from Rome in Otacilia's name which mark the Saecular
Games include the following reverse inscriptions:

MILIARVM SAECVLVM: *cippus / As* and *Sestertius* (RIC IV 199)
SAECVLARES AVGG: hippopotamus / *Sestertius* (RIC IV 200)
SAECVLARES AVGG: elk walking left / *Sestertius* (RIC IV 201)[337]

---

334 Bland, 2014, Cat. 37.

335 It is interesting to note that the Egyptian deity Tawaret, who took the form of a hippopotamus,
     was a deity of fertility and associated with birth and rebirth. It may have been an appropriate, if
     unusual, link to the new Golden Age; Capel and Markoe, 1996, 132.

336 Whetstone, 1978, 26.

337 Figure 46.

SAECVLARES AVGG:	*cippus* /*Aureus* (RIC IV 117)/ *As*,[338]
	Sestertius (RIC 199, 202)
SAECVLVM NOVVM:	hexastyle temple with *Roma* (RIC IV
	118, *Aureus*)

The SAECVLARES AVGG coinage of Philip II

Philip II was probably given the title Caesar when he was seven years old and elevated to Augustus in AD 247 at the age of nine.[339] The Saecular games coinage issued from Rome, includes issues with the reverse inscription SAECVLARES AVGG and the image of an animal which is usually described as a goat (Figure 47).

Figure 47: Radiate of Phillip II (RIC IV 224) © Private collection

The Sestertii of Philip II show similar animals, also generally described as goats, on the basis of the short horns and a bearded chin (Figure 48).

Figure 48: Sestertius of Philip II (RIC IV 264a) © CNG Auction Triton X, Lot 726, January 2007

However, the animal here has a bulbous nose and bifurcated horns and also appears on the reverse of coins of Otacilia Severa (Figure 46).

The passage quoted above from the *SHA*, which lists the animals for Philip's games, includes *alces decem*, (ten elk). So rather than goats these are much more likely to be elk or moose which were identified among the exotic animals seen in the Saecular Games. [340]

338 Figure 31.
339 Southern, 2001, 92.
340 Twente, 1978, 56.

The iconography of the Golden Age in the Aion Mosaic at Philippopolis

To celebrate the Saecular Games was to affirm the return of a Golden Age through cyclical time, a concept which included belief in complex astrology, as outlined in the introduction. The main contemporary written source for the mid third century, the Thirteenth Sybilline Oracle, includes this passage which refers to the cities which Philip I enhanced in his native land and emphasises the link that Philip and these cities have to astrology and the zodiac circle:

> *"Now be adorned, cities of Arabia, with temples and stadia and market places and fora and splendidly shining wealth and images in gold, silver and ivory; and most of all Bostra, though you be pre-eminent among them all in astrology, and Philippopolis, so that you will not come to grief. The resounding spheres of the zodiac circle will not profit you, nor the Ram, the Bull, the Gemini nor as many other ascendant stars as appear with them in heaven; alas you will have placed great trust in them by the time your day shall finally come."* [341]

As recorded by Aurelius Victor, Philip I founded the city of Philippopolis, probably on or near the site of his birth at Shahba in Syria, in AD 244.[342] This city clearly enjoyed imperial patronage and extant buildings include the so-called *"Philippeion"* which may have been a mausoleum for Philip's deified father, Julius Marinus. [343]

The lines quoted from the Sybilline Oracle come directly after the passage connected with the Millennial Games, discussed in the written sources above. It has been suggested that the mention of astrology and the zodiac circle may be taken as "a reference to an imperial building programme at Philippopolis in which astral imagery may have played a part".[344]

---

341 Potter D, 1990, 171.
342 Victor, *Liber De Caesaribus*, 28.
343 Butcher, 2003, 234.
344 Amer and Gawlikowski, 1985, 15.

Figure 49: Aion mosaic from Philippopolis, Damascus Museum, Syria © G Barker (courtesy of M Nazha)

One of a series of elaborate mosaics from Philippopolis, probably dating from the mid to late third century, includes a depiction of Aion holding a zodiacal wheel (Figure 49). Alföldi identified Aion as "an allegory of the powers of the emperors responsible for the return to the Golden Age, as a means of political propaganda".[345]

The "Aion mosaic" depicts a number of mythical figures, many of whom are connected to the fruitfulness of the earth and the concept of cyclical time. In the centre of the mosaic sits *Ge* (Earth) accompanied by four children identified as *Karpoi* (fruits of the earth).[346] Prometheus fashions the first man to Ge's left whilst Aion sits on her right holding his zodiacal wheel. Behind Aion stand the four seasons. All the themes in the mosaic can be seen as aspects of cyclical change.[347] Chapter 5.2 below explores the iconography of Aion on imperial coinage.

The Aion mosaic from Philippopolis may represent an adaptation of Hellenistic myths that had been re-articulated and re-presented in the context of Roman beliefs current in Arabia in the mid-third century AD. One of the main themes of the mosaic is the eternity of the cosmic cycle.[348] The mosaic

---

345 Bijovsky, 2007,152; Alfoldi,1997, 135-163.

346 See Chapter 5.1 for the similar "mother earth" figure of Tellus.

347 Cohen, 2014, 17.

348 Quet, 2000,183.

can also been as an illustration of the Golden Age which celebrates the good government of the emperor guaranteeing peace and prosperity.[349] In short, "Philip sought to link his own dynastic claims of the eternity of Rome and the beginning of a new Golden Age, ideas that seemed to have influenced the content of the Philippopolis mosaic."[350]

Summary

The coinage issued to commemorate Philip's Saecular Games in AD 248 tend to confirm that Augustan precedents were followed to usher in a new Golden Age at Rome's millennium. The dated *cippus* coinage, this time with the inscription SAECVLARES AVGG, proclaimed that the imperial family all took part in the Saecular Games rituals and follows the design set by Augustus. These coins were produced in greater numbers than before but are still comparatively rare. Rare medallions (Figures 32 and 33) show the emperor sacrificing at a Saecular Games ceremony and are similar to coin images produced by Domitian (Figure 4) and Septimius Severus (Figure 11). These medallions were probably intended for circulation to a small number of the elite ruling circle.

As befits a millennial celebration, lower value coinage was produced in greater quantities than before and must have been intended for a wider circulation. These radiates mostly displayed images of animals from the Saecular Games. These were images that could be understood at a broad level, as could the image and inscription of *Roma Aeterna*, the deity associated with Philip's Saecular Games.

The Thirteenth Sybilline oracle and the Aion mosaic from Philippopolis (Figure 49) may provide evidence that Philip espoused the idea of a Golden Age returning through cyclical time. The reverse inscription of SAECVLVM NOVVM on some issues (Figures 41-43) is corroborative evidence for this. There is no reason to doubt that Philip I used the Golden Age myth as legitimation for his reign, as Augustus, Septimius Severus and others had done before him.

2.3   The *SAECVLVM NOVVM* coinage of emperors following Philip I

The iconography established by Philip I for his *saecvlvm novvm* coinage was continued by the two emperors who succeeded him. Trajan Decius (AD 249-151) also claimed he was the emperor bringing a new Golden Age as is indicated by the image of the temple of *Roma Aeterna* with the reverse inscription SAECVLVM NOVVM. This design appeared on coins of his wife, Herennia Etruscilla[351] and his son Hostilian (Figure 50).

---

349   La Rocca, 1984, 84.
350   Parrish, 1995, 167–190.
351   RIC IV 67c.

Figure 50: Radiate of Hostilian (RIC IV 199b) © Private collection

In common with so many third century emperors, Trajan Decius was keen to affirm the traditional role of Roman religion. It was probably this that motivated him to issue his famous edict which required a recordable sacrifice to the principal gods of the Roman Empire.[352] The Christian communities demonised the emperor for this edict,[353] which has been described as not only the best recorded event in the third century AD but possibly the best attested government action in the whole of antiquity. [354]

Trebonianus Gallus (AD 251-253) was also to claim the return of a Golden Age and issued coins with the same reverse design of *Roma Aeterna* and the reverse inscription SAECVLLVM NOVVM (Figure 51). Volusian, the emperor's son and co-ruler also issued radiates (*antoniniani*) from Antioch with the same design. Coins were issued with the inscription SAECVLVM NOVVM[355] and SAECVLLVM NOVVM. [356]

Figure 51: Radiate of Trebonianus Gallus (RIC IV 90) © Private collection

For each emperor, the claim to Golden Age of stability and peace proved to be hollow. Philip, Trajan Decius and Trebonianus Gallus were all assassinated after a relatively short period of rule. In addition to the impact of the Millennial Games, it is also possible that the extraordinary emphasis on Golden Age claims by these emperors may have been connected with the religious tensions that abounded during this period.[357]

352 Fowden, 2005, 557.
353 Brent, 2009, 261.
354 Ando, 2012, 122.
355 RIC IV 235.
356 RIC IV 236.
357 Potter, 1990, 39.

3

THE GOLDEN AGE ICONOGRAPHY OF THE COINAGE OF GALLIENUS AND THE TETRARCHY

3.1 The coinage of Gallienus

Gallienus and a new spirituality?

"Gallienus became Augustus as a young man and at the beginning of his reign he ruled the empire favourably, then he ruled well, but at the end calamitously." [358]

As this quotation from Eutropius illustrates, the majority of later written sources are hostile to Gallienus and aspects of his reign remain controversial.[359] He reigned jointly with Valerian from AD 253-260 and then as sole ruler from AD 260 – 268. During this time he presided over a particularly troubled period of the Roman Empire. The number of natural disasters, wars and rebellions was never higher; added to which, his reign witnessed a series of plagues and an economic collapse. His father Valerian I (AD 253-260) had set out to emphasise the traditional rituals of Roman religion in order to return to peace and prosperity,[360] but Valerian's reign ended in the disaster of his capture and murder by Shapur; an ignominious and deeply humiliating event in Roman annals. [361]

Valerian had issued two edicts, in AD 257 and 258, enforcing traditional Roman religious observance[362] which ultimately resulted in the martyrdom, amongst others, of St Cyprian.[363] One of the first acts of Gallienus, however, appears to have been to restore to the Christian bishops their rights over church

---

358 *"Gallienus, cum adulescens factus esset Augustus, imperium primum feliciter, mox commode, ad ultimum perniciose gessit."* Eutropius, *Breviarum*, IX.8; (translation G Barker).

359 Cf. Zonaras, Book XII, 24/25 who is more favourable to Gallienus.

360 Southern, 2015, 101.

361 Eutropius, *Breviarum*, Book IX.7.

362 Eusebius, *Historia Ecclesiastica*, 7.11.6-11.

363 Brent, 2010, 20.

property and greater freedom of worship.[364] Gallienus may have put the role of emperor on a higher spiritual plane and identified himself with a greater number of deities, as protectors and companions, than ever before.[365] One surviving inscription from Ostia reads:

"To the unconquerable, pious, fortunate Augustus Gallienus who is like the gods in thought and appearance" [366]

This unique inscription may serve to emphasise his interest in and his identification with the divine.

Gallienus and Salonina may have taken an interest in the neoplatonic philosophy of Plotinus.[367] Porphyry mentions that Sabinillus, described as an assiduous student of Plotinus, served as consul with Gallienus in AD 266 and also describes a major project to found a community for Plotinus in Campania to be called *"Platonopolis."* [368] This project never came to fruition, it appears, because of opposition at Court and Gallienus's untimely death.[369]

The significance which Gallienus attached to Neoplatonism or Christianity is unclear and may reflect partly a natural curiosity in contemporary thought and partly a pragmatic approach to garner support from different constituents at the time.[370]

It has been convincingly argued that Gallienus was initiated into the Eleusinian mysteries on a visit to Athens in September AD 264.[371] During this visit, he was also elected *archon*,[372] as Hadrian had been, over a century before him. As well as confirming his Philhellene leanings, this also tends to confirm Gallienus's interest in traditional rituals. In the early 260s, Gallienus is thought to have built the so-called Arch of Gallienus (Figure 52). This was an appropriation of a gate built by Augustus and stands as one indication among many that Gallienus wanted to emulate Augustus as the bringer of a Golden Age.[373]

---

364 Eusebius, *Historia Ecclesiastica*, 7.13.1.

365 De Blois, 1976, 159.

366 *"Invicto Imperatori Pio Felici Gallieno Augusto dis animo voltuque compare"* ILS 550 CIL XIV 5334 (translation G. Barker).

367 Ousager, 2004, 314; Porphyry, Life of Plotinus, 12.

368 Porphyry, Life of Plotinus, 7 and 12.

369 De Blois, 1994, 173.

370 De Blois, 1976, 185.

371 Armstrong, 1987, 235 – 258.

372 *SHA*, Gallienus, 11.3.

373 Hedlund, 2008, 128; De Blois, 1976, 129.

Figure 52: The "Arch of Gallienus", Via di S. Vito, Rome © G Barker 2019

The iconography on coinage of Gallienus and Salonina linked to Golden Age themes

Considering the enormous upheaval during his time in power, it might have been expected that a ritual such as the Saecular Games would have been celebrated by Gallienus to invoke the peace and prosperity so desperately sought at that time. The coins issued by Gallienus include the typical generic Golden Age type legends which are common in the third century AD, such as *pax* [374] and *uberitas*.[375] They also display more unusual inscriptions such as *ubique pax* on a series of *aurei*, minted at Rome in AD 266/7.[376]

Firm claims have been made that Gallienus celebrated the Saecular Games towards the end of his reign.[377] The main evidence for this is numismatic. For example, there are the radiates minted in Antioch (Figures 53 and 54) and Rome with the reverse inscription SAECVLARES or SAECVLARHS AVG (the second E appears as an H in a Greek hyper-correction). These coins echo the reverse inscription on the Saecular Games coinage of Philip I, discussed above.

---

374 E.g. RIC V 87.

375 E.g. RIC V 71.

376 E.g. RIC V 74 where the obverse shows Gallienus with a *corona spicea* (crown of wheat ears) which may link to Ceres in the *Carmen Saeculare* (De Blois, 1976, 130). The obverse inscription appears to be feminine (though it could be vocative) and may show Gallienus as Demeter restoring peace (De Blois, 1976, 126).

377 Toynbee, 1986, 163, note 171; Cerfaux Tondriaux, 1957, 376.

Figure 53: Radiate of Gallienus (RIC V 1 656) © British Museum: 2006,0606,469

The reverse design of the SAECVLARES AVG coinage depicts the stag of Diana, and this highlights a distinctive aspect in the coinage of Gallienus. The coin designs throughout his reign strongly feature Apollo and Diana. They had also featured in the coinage of his father Valerian. [378]

Figure 54: Radiate of Gallienus (RIC V 1 656) © Münzkabinet der Staatlichen Museen zu Berlin: 18200678

Apollo and Diana were key to the Augustan Saecular Games and the Augustan Golden Age,[379] with Horace's *Carmen Saeculare* being addressed to these deities.[380] It has also been argued by Miller that it was Diana's role in winning key battles for Augustus[381] that led to his adopting the goddess alongside Apollo. Diana therefore appealed to later emperors in the context of successful warfare. Diana features on a series of coins and medallions in the second century AD, issued by emperors who saw themselves as "the new

---

378 e,g, RIC V 114 and 115.

379 De Blois, 1976, 130. Forsyth, 2012,73; Miller, 2009, 270; see the introduction.

380 See Appendix II; Horace, *Carmen Saeculare*, lines 1,2,15.

381 Especially the battle of Naulochus in 3 BC; see Miller, 2009, 22; Augustan coinage with Diana includes: RIC 172, 173, 175, 181-183, 194-197, 204.

Augusti." [382] In emulation of Augustus, both Hadrian[383] and Antoninus Pius[384] issued medallions and coins depicting Diana.[385]

Gallienus can therefore be seen in this tradition of presenting himself as a second Augustus by adopting Diana not only as a deity for successful warfare but also a goddess associated with a new Golden Age.

The SAECVLARES AVG coins do not feature in large numbers in coin hoards. So, for example, the Qula hoard contains 6 of these coins out of a total of 1,023 coins for the sole reign of Gallienus (0.5%).[386]

Gallienus even issued coins with the legend DEO AVGVSTO on the occasion of his *Decennalia* in AD 262 (Figure 55).[387] The coins of Gallienus with the description of Augustus as a god are very rare (five examples only are known) and are regarded as unprecedented on imperial coinage.[388]

Figure 55: Aureus of Gallienus (RIC 9) © Wildwinds image

Both Valerian and Gallienus also issued coinage with an image of the god Saturn, who is shown as an older bearded man with a covered head. Virgil associated Saturn with the curved sickle or falx e.g. *curvo Saturni dente* (the curved blade of Saturn)[389] providing him with a recognisable emblem.[390] For Valerian the reverse inscription was AETERNITATI AVGG (the eternity of the Augusti).[391] On the coinage of Gallienus, with the same iconography, the inscription is AETERNITAS AVG (Figure 56). This coinage continues the

---

382 Toynbee, 1986, 140; Abdy, 2019,37.

383 E.g. RIC II 147.

384 E.g. Gnecchi III 136,27.

385 For iconography of Artemis/ Diana see LIMC I, 151-271.

386 Kool, 2016, 69-118.

387 The issue is reminiscent of the CONSECRATIO series issued by Trajan Decius of eleven deified emperors, including Augustus (RIC IV 3 117- 118 and 130-132).

388 Calomino, 2015, 73.

389 Virgil, Georgics II, 406.

390 For other images of Saturn see the wall painting of Saturn from the House of the Dioscuri, Naples, *Museo Archeologico Nazionale* (from Pompeii, *Casa dei Dioscuri* (VI, 9, 6-7) and the central panel from the mosaic from El Jem (Tunis Musée National du Bardo A 10); LIMC VIII Saturnus 1078-1089.

391 RIC V 210.

Golden Age message linked to Saturn and the Virgilian *Saturnia regna* (reign of Saturn).[392] As discussed in the introduction, the Golden Age of Augustus becomes the Age of Saturn.[393] In the Qula hoard, this coin represented just over 4% of the coins of Gallienus.

Figure 56: Radiate of Gallienus (RIC V 606) © CNG E-sale 241 Lot 525 September 2010

Salonina's coinage displays the general iconography of Golden Age images of peace and plenty. In particular, coins with a reverse inscription of FECVNDITAS show Salonina with two children, emphasising dynastic continuity (Figure 57). It has been suggested by Alföldi that the mass issue of coins with this reverse legend from nine *officinae* in AD 265 probably coincided with the birth of Marinianus, the third son of Gallienus and Salonina.[394]

Figure 57: Aureus of Salonina (RIC V I5) © British Museum: 1874,0714.4

The iconography of the 'Animal Series' coinage

An intriguing series of coins includes representations of Apollo and Diana. These issues, from the mints of Rome and Siscia, are known as the "animal series" in honour of nine particular deities and represented by animals closely associated with them.[395] The reverse inscription on these coins is an abbreviation

392 De Blois,1976, p 129.
393 See discussion in the Introduction.
394 Alfoldi, 1929, 267.
395 Wiegel, 1990, 135 -143.

of CONSERVATOR AVGVSTI. This title recognises the named god as a special protector of the emperor.[396] Whilst the coins of the third century AD witnessed a small number of additional gods identified as an emperor's protector, it was only Gallienus who used this epithet with such an extensive list of deities.

Various associations have been made between this series of coins and the Golden Age myth, though interpretations remain hypothetical.[397] It is possible these coins are connected with the conflict between Gallienus and Postumus that developed around AD 265 and represent an "armoury" of traditional gods who would protect Rome in the war against "The Gallic Empire".[398] Given the range of coins connected with Golden Age themes produced by Postumus[399] it may be there was an element of competition as to which emperor was bringing back the Golden Age which underlay rival claims for legitimacy.[400]

The nine gods celebrated on Galienus' coins are: Apollo, Diana, Hercules, Jupiter, Juno, Liber Pater, Mercury, Neptune and Sol. Of these, Apollo and Diana feature particularly heavily in the series as they did throughout Gallienus's reign, including his joint rule with his father Valerian.[401]

In this series, Apollo is represented on the reverse either by a centaur (Figure 58) or a griffin, and the reverse inscription is APOLLINI CONS AVG. Diana's prominence is emphasised by being accorded the greatest variety of animals in this series. The animals representing Diana include a doe (Figure 59), a stag, an antelope, a goat and a boar. These animals came under Diana's protection as goddess of the hunt.[402]

Figure 58: Radiate of Gallienus (RIC V 1 163) © CNG image ref: 158142

396 De Blois, 1976, 160.
397 See Weigel, *op. cit.* for the various possible Golden Age links. He suggests Diana and Apollo may have been represented in their roles as protectors of health as the plague was so common at this time; this may link to the purificatory aspects of the Saecular Games. Also, five of these deities, Apollo, Diana, Mercury, Neptune and Hercules were associated with the consultation of the Sybilline books.
398 Hedlund, 2008, 214.
399 E.g. RIC V -2, 263 (Mairat No. 372) showing Jugate busts of Apollo and Diana.
400 Manders, 2012, 295 and 307. Both Postumus and Gallienus claimed association with Hercules.
401   e.g. RIC V 114 and 115.
402 Wiegel,1990, 137; the goat may represent an animal for sacrifice to Diana.

Of the 2,737 coins from the 'animal series' in the Cunetio hoard, over 40% (1,190) make reference to Diana. About 20% (543) of the coins in this hoard represented Apollo.[403]

Figure 59: Radiate of Gallienus (RIC V 1 176) © *Private collection*

Sol is represented either by a winged horse (Figure 60) or a bull in the 'animal series'. Horace's *Carmen Saeculare* contains direct references to Sol.[404] Sol was also the protector of chariot races in the Circus Maximus, one of the featured elements of the Saecular Games, [405] and the circuit of the Circus may have represented the nature of cyclical time and the *saeculum* itself. [406]

Figure 60: Radiate of Gallienus (RIC V 283) © *CNG image ref: 784022*

The nine gods represented in the 'animal series' are, for the most part, ancient protectors of Rome who have antecedents in the Greek pantheon. The exception to this is Sol, whose presence may be explained by his association with Apollo. Geiger has suggested that Gallienus may have been inspired by the animals that Philip I displayed on his Saecular Games coinage.[407] It is also possible these coins represent a major religious festival which included

---

403 Forsyth, 2012, 55; Livy, *Historia Romae* 7.2; Zosimus 2.1.1.

404 Hijmans, 2009, 549-566; Horace, *Carmen Saeculare*, lines 9-12; see Appendix II.

405 See Figure 35.

406 Forsyth, 2012, 128; Abdy, 2019, 38.

407 Geiger, 2013, 235.

a display of animals[408] though it remains open to question whether there is evidence for a celebration of the Saecular Games.[409]

The Golden Age iconography of Amalthea on the coinage of Gallienus and his sons

For the first few years of Gallienus's joint rule with his father Valerian from AD 253, it must have seemed that the greatly desired stability of a true dynastic succession was in place. The combination of Golden Age fruitfulness combined with an image of dynasty has already been noted on the coinage of his wife Salonina. Gallienus and Salonina produced three sons which, at the time, must have seemed a reasonable guarantee for the continuance of the dynasty.

The eldest son was Valerian II, who was awarded the title of Caesar in AD 255 or 256[410] though, tragically, he was to die within a couple of years. Fewer than sixty coin types of his are recorded by RIC but the most distinctive reverses incorporate the inscription IOVI CRESCENTI with an image of the young Jupiter on the back of the goat, generally identified as that of Amalthea (Figure 61).[411] These were struck in Rome[412] and a mint in northern Europe, probably Lugdunum[413], as radiates (*antoniniani*) and *aurei*. The coins of Valerian II are comparatively common and in the Cunetio hoard, coins from the mint of Gaul with this reverse legend comprise 11% of the coins of Valerian II.

Figure 61: Radiate of Valerian II (RIC V 3) © Private collection

The depiction of Amalthea was not new. A coin of 85 BC is thought to show the infant Jupiter on the back of Amalthea.[414] Medallions with the image of Amalthea had been produced by Hadrian[415] and Antoninus Pius (Figure 62).

408 Weigel,1990, 140.
409 De Blois, 1976, 128.
410 Southern, 2001, 100.
411 LIMC I, 437-438.
412 RIC V 1,13-17.
413 RIC V 1, 1 and 3.
414 *Denarius* of Fonteius, Crawford 353/1a; child has wings and is sometimes described as Veiovis. This design was later copied by Titus with Domitian's head on the obverse and the reverse inscription PRINCEPS IVVENTVTIS (the first amongst the young: ie. the heir) RIC II 267.
415 RIC II 670 var.

Figure 62: Medallion of Antoninus Pius (Gnecchi, 1912, III p27/135)© British Museum: 1937,0607.88

The messianic child, or '*nascens puer*' in line 49 of Virgil's Fourth *Eclogue*, is described as the "*magnus Iovis incrementum*" (great progeny of Jove). This is an allusion to the offspring of Jupiter or Jupiter having been born again.[416] Diodorus Siculus, amongst other writers, records the myth of the young Jupiter being reared by the she-goat Amalthea.[417] This has been identified as a reference to a new Golden Age with the young Caesar as guarantor of the *novum saeculum*.[418] In other words, the crown-prince is represented as "the bringer of the Golden Age." [419]

The horn of Amalthea is also associated with the cornucopia (horn of plenty),[420] as the child was supplied with an abundant supply of milk from one of the broken horns. [421] The cornucopia had been a symbol of abundance long before Augustus, so it no surprise to find it associated with his Golden Age. [422] Indeed, the cornucopia has been described as "a leitmotif in Augustan literature and iconography".[423] Horace's *Carmen Saeculare* includes the line "Blessed Plenty dares to appear again, now with her flowing horn" [424] and the goddess Tellus, often associated with the Augustan Golden Age imagery, is usually depicted carrying a cornucopia.[425]

At the same time as the coins for Valerian II were minted, the Lugdunum mint also issued coins in the name of Gallienus with the reverse design of

---

416 Mattingly, 1947, 18-19; MacMullen, 1967, 333; See Morrell, Osgood & Welch, 2019, 110 for the idea that the *puer* is a metaphor for the dawn of new day.

417 Diodorus Siculus, *Bibliotecha Historica*, V 71; cf. Ovid *Fasti* V, III-128 where Amalthea is the name of a nymph who has charge of the goat. See discussion in Gee, 2000, 126-140.

418 Grandvallet, 2006, 140; McMullen, 1966, 333; de Blois, 1976, 134.

419 Alföldi, 1929, 270.

420 Diodorus Siculus, *Bibliotecha Hisorica*, IV, 35.3.

421 Roberts, 1998, 19.

422 Galinsky, 1996, 106.For example of an Augustan coin with Pax and cornucopia see: RIC I 252.

423 Gee, 2000, 135.

424 "*beata pleno copia cornu*": Horace, *Carmen Saeculare*, lines 59-60. (Translation by A. Kline) See Appendix II.

425 See Chapter 5.1.

the child Jupiter riding Amalthea and the inscription IOVI CRESCENTI.[426] A similar design can be found on Roman gems as in Figure 64.[427] A mint in northern Europe, probably Viminacium, issued rare coins with the same design but with the reverse description LAETIT TEMP, abbreviated from LAETITIA TEMPORVM (Figure 63).

Figure 63: Radiate of Gallienus (RIC V 384) © British Museum: 1995,0703.17

Figure 64: Roman Glass Intaglio © British Museum: 1814,0704.2594

A rare contemporary issue from Mediolanum also shows the child Jupiter suckling Amalthea but with the reverse inscription PIET SAECVLI (Figure 65). Pietas was one of the key virtues for Augustus [428] and the use of the word *saeculi* in conjunction with this image underlines the return of the Golden Age through cyclical time.

Figure 65: Radiate of Gallienus (RIC V 393/394) Pecunem Auction August 2013, Lot 572

426 RIC V 20.
427 Toynbee cites a fresco of Amalthea from the *Domus Aurea* in Rome: Toynbee, 1973, 166.
428 Galinsky, 1996, 88.

The hopes of continuing the dynasty that were pinned on Valerian II were dashed with his death in AD 258. He was probably killed in the revolt of Ingenuus at Cologne.[429] The year AD 260 was the most tragic for Gallienus as not only did he lose his son Saloninus[430] but also his father Valerian was captured by Shapur.

At around this time, Gallienus chose to claim descent from the *gens* Valeria by emphasising the line of his mother's family who were from Falerii in Etruria.[431] This was a significant link for an emperor who wanted to bring back a Golden Age as by ancient tradition, the *gens* Valeria were celebrated as the family that had instituted the Saecular Games.[432] An inscription survives from Falerii which is dedicated to Gallienus and Salonina.[433] Medallions in gold and silver were struck in Rome featuring Gallienus and Salonina on the obverse with a reverse inscription of PIETAS FALERI and design of a goat suckling a child[434] with a second child to the right (Figure 66).

Figure 66: Silver Medallion of Gallienus and Salonin (Gnecchi, 1912, I, p54/1)
© Kunsthistorisches Museum Vienna RÖ 32268

429 Southern, 2001, 100.
430 Possibly named after the son of Pollio to whom Virgil's Fourth *Eclogue* was dedicated (Mattingly, 1947, 18, and Alfoldi, 1929, 265). Cf. *SHA, Gallieni Duo*, IXX.3 and *SHA, Gallieni Duo*, XX1.3.
431 Coins and medallions were issued with the reverse inscription VIRTUS FALERI which showed Gallienus as Hercules (e.g. RIC V 596). See discussion on *virtus* in a Golden Age context in Chapter 6. See Manders, 2012, 295.
432 See introduction; Zosimus, 2 1-3; Mineo, 2015, 396; Versnel,1994, 323.
433 CIL XI 3089.
434 RIC V 1 & 2.

In order to clarify the identity of the child being suckled by the goat, Jupiter's eagle appears on the right and in the exergue is a thunderbolt. The tree could be a *topos* indicative of a mythological scene or it could represent the fecundity of the Golden Age.[435] The child with the baby Jupiter is probably Saloninus, shown as the heir apparent destined to bring back the Golden Age.[436] This medallion appears to present the reign of Gallienus as the start of a new era by using the Golden Age imagery of Amalthea and the child Jupiter.

Summary

Gallienus produced coinage with iconography that is highly original in many respects. The novel designs may reflect his aim to legitimise his position by placing the emperor in a closer relationship with a wide range of deities. Alongside this new spirituality, Gallienus wanted to be seen as a new Augustus who was the bringer of a new Golden Age of peace. This can be seen firstly in the portrayal of Valerian II as a new progeny of Jupiter in the Virgilian Golden Age spirit. Then, even after the disasters of the deaths of his father and two eldest sons, Gallienus continued to present his own version of the Augustan Golden Age myth as a bringer of peace and prosperity. In this context, he emphasised the ancient Etruscan lineage of his mother's family by inscribing coins and medallions with references to Faleri, [437] and the familiar combination of Golden Age imagery and dynastic messages appear on these coins and medallions.

One of the most striking aspects of the coinage of Gallienus is the emphasis on Apollo and Diana as the CONSERVATORES (special protectors) of his reign, with Diana being featured very heavily. The mysterious "animal series" coinage underscores the importance that Gallienus attached to Apollo and Diana, who were key to the Augustan Saecular Games, but any precise link to a Golden Age myth remains elusive.

Whilst the Gallienus coins with reverse inscriptions of SAECVLARES AVG are typical of the Saecular Games issues of Philip I, the dated *cippus*, the coin design which provides the main evidence that the rituals took place, is not recorded for Gallienus's reign. This would tend to support the argument that Gallienus was planning to hold the Saecular Games but never, in fact, celebrated them.[438] Nevertheless, with so many allusions to the Augustan Golden Age on his coinage, the reasonable claim has been made that Gallienus "may have deliberately resuscitated, in new forms, the 'Golden Age' mysticism of the first *princeps*." [439]

---

435 See the discussion in the context of Tellus in Chapter 5.1.
436 Alföldi, 1929, 273.
437 e.g. RIC V 596.
438 De Blois, 1976, 128.
439 Grant, 1950, 136.

3.2 The Coinage of the Tetrarchy

The Written sources

Oxyrhynchus papyri

> *"Capitoline Zeus took pity at last on the human race and gave the lordship of all the earth and the sea to godlike king Diocletian.........*
> *The whole land takes delight in its joy as at the light of a Golden Age; and iron, drawn back from the slaughter of men, lies bloodlessly in its scabbard."* [440]

This excerpt of verse, which is translated from one of the Oxyrhynchus papyri from Egypt, may have been composed for the celebration of the Capitoline Games in AD 285, shortly after Diocletian became emperor.[441] The reference to the Golden Age myth on the departure of an age of iron is clear. Such poetic proclamations heralding the arrival of a Golden Age might not be regarded as particularly unusual, except that Diocletian's reign saw the successful establishment of a new regime based on "a more absolutist monarchy".[442]

Despite a ruthlessly practical approach, Diocletian's accession included a story that made it appear he was following a prophetic destiny. He had killed Aper, the murderer of Numerianus, in front of the troops and claimed this fulfilled a prophecy of a female seer in Gaul who had told him he would be emperor after slaying a boar (*aper* in Latin).[443] It is also recorded that he quoted Virgil when carrying out this execution saying that Aper could boast, *"I fell by the mighty hand of Aeneas".*[444]

The so-called Arch of Galerius, dating from around AD 298, includes a panel of Diocletian and Galerius making a sacrifice (Figure 67). The figure on the extreme left in this picture, under a zodiacal circle, represents Aion, the god of cyclical time, who is depicted in many images as the bringer of the Golden Age[445] (see Chapter 5.2).

---

440 P. Oxy. LXIII 4352 (translation: John Rea).
441 Rea, 1996, 214; Cameron, 2016,16.
442 Bowman, CHA 2005, 67.
443 Zonaras, Book XII, 31; *SHA*, Carus, 14. Robert Adam recorded a frieze, no longer extant, in Diocletian's Palace at Split showing a boar being killed which may refer to this prophecy: Adam, 1764, Plate LI.
444 *"Aeneae magni dextra cadi"* (translation G. Barker): *SHA, Carus,* 13.
445 Leadbetter, 2009, 96; Rothman, 1977, 440.

Figure 67: Detail from the Arch of Galerius (c AD 298) Salonica, Image from Featurepics

The reign of Diocletian and his fellow rulers[446] continued to see an outpouring of writings as a product of the "third century spiritual explosion".[447] Porphyry and St Cyprian can be seen as two of the main writers in the search for spiritual truth in this period. The problems that arose with new beliefs being formed at this time can be glimpsed in Diocletian's edict against the Manicheans. In this edict the emperor shows himself as a vigorous defender of traditional Roman beliefs:

> " *But the immortal gods in their providence have seen fit to ordain that what is good and true should be judged and held as sacrosanct by the counsel and deliberation of many good, distinguished and very wise men. It is a serious crime to challenge or oppose these solid principles, based on ancient beliefs, and which are firmly held and have current vailidity .*" [448]

446 The term Tetrarchy for this period was a nineteenth century invention. See Leadbetter, 2009, 3-6.
447 Leadbetter, 2009, 124.
448 *Sed dii immortales prouidentia sua ordinare et disponere dignati sunt, quae bona et uera sunt ut multorum et bonorum et egregiorum uirorum et sapientissimorum consilio et tractatu inlibata probarentur et statuerentur, quibus nec obuiam ire nec resistere fas est, neque reprehendi a noua uetus religio deberet. maximi enim criminis est retractare quae semel ab antiquis statuta et definita suum statum et cursum tenent ac possident:* Coll. 15.3.2; (Translation G Barker); see Gardner and Lieu, 2004, 117.

The Panegyrics

Golden Age references are to be found in the *Panegyrici Latini*, the elaborate court speeches from the late Empire.[449] A specific use of the Golden Age myth occurs in a speech by Eumenius, which is essentially about the restoration of a city in Gaul or Germania (possibly Augustadunum or Mogantiacum). It is estimated that this speech dates from the late 290s AD. In the context of a passage about the re-establishment of army bases and troops along the Rhine, the following statement is to be found:

> *"Thus, in actual fact, that Golden Age which once briefly flourished when Saturn was king is now reborn under the eternal auspices of Jupiter and Hercules."* [450]

Jupiter and Hercules refer directly to Diocletian and Maximian through their adopted patron deities with whom they were closely identified.[451] It is, of course, highly appropriate to place a Golden Age reference in the middle of a speech about renewal. This is a particularly distinctive passage, and unusual in the panegyrics, as it talks specifically about the rebirth of a Golden Age and the former age of Saturn.

These are Virgilian allusions[452] and the context of this reference, in a passage describing renewed military strength, echoes the Augustan theme of a Golden Age peace achieved through armed supremacy.[453] Just as Septimius Severus added his patron deities to his Saecular games coin design, so the patron deities of Diocletian and Maximian have been added to this Golden Age passage.

Other Virgilian references can be identified in the panegyrics, such as the phrase *"Jovis Omnia Esse"* (of Jove all things are full)[454] in a panegyric to Maximian which is taken from Virgil's Third *Eclogue*. [455] The panegyrics

---

449 Hardie, 1986, 257-259; Nixon and Rodgers, 1994,26-33.

450 *"Adeo, ut res est, aurea illa saecula, quae non diu quondam Saturno rege viguerent, nunc aeternis auspicis Iovis and Herculis renascuntur."* Eumenius, *Panegyrici Latini*, IX, 18; Nixon and Rodgers, 1994, 170.

451 As part of a new legitimation of power that was rooted in Roman tradition: Lo Cascio, 2005, 171.

452 *"Augustus Caesar, divi genus, aurea condet/ Saecula qui rursus Latio regnata per arva/ Saturno quondam."* (Augustus Caesar, son of a god, who will again establish a Golden Age in Latium amid fields once ruled by Saturn); Virgil, *Aeneid*, VI 792-794; (translation: H R Fairclough). For further Virgilian references see de la Bédoyère, 1998, 82.

453 Ware, 2012, 196; Rantala, 2013, 14.

454 *Genethliacus Maximiani Augusti*, 14.2; Nixon and Rodgers, 1993, 98. Virgil, in turn, is quoting from Aratus, *Phaenomena* 1.

455 *"Ab Iove principium Musae, Iovis omnia plena; ille colit terras, illi mea carmina curae"* (Jove is my main inspiration; all things are full of of Jove. It is he who makes the earth bountiful; it is he who motivates my writing of verses). Virgil *Eclogues*, 3.60 (translation: G Barker). This in turn is derived from Aratus, *Phaenomena*, 1.

were written for the emperor, his courtiers and imperial officials who might be described as an educated elite and, if performed, they were presented on special occasions.[456] The panegyrics may have been part of the process of self-legitimation that this this book claims for the coins with Golden Age iconography. Indeed, in the context of later panegyrics, it has been claimed "panegyricists sought to impress on the Roman elite the legitimacy and success of their rulers." [457]

The close links between Tetrarchic coinage from Lugdunum and the panegyrics have been analysed[458] and these detailed studies tend to confirm that, in this period, imperial coins were "an official document and, as such, represented an official expression of the emperor and his regime." [459]

Zosimus

Zosimus writes extensively about the Saecular Games. In this section of his history he includes a curious comment about Maximian:

> " From the consulate of Chilo and Libo, in which Severus celebrated the saecular games, to the ninth consulate of Diocletian, and eighth of Maximian, was a hundred and one years. Maximian wished to celebrate the festival at that time, contrary to rule, but in the following year Diocletian became a private citizen, instead of emperor, and Maximian followed his example." [460]

It has been deduced from this passage, and from a reference to the thousandth anniversary of Rome in the panegyric to Maximian and Constantine, that Maximian celebrated the Saecular Games in AD 304.[461] However, Zosimus creates doubt about this, so any Saecular celebration may have taken place earlier.

The coinage of the Tetrarchy

Whilst Golden Age references can be found in the rhetoric of the Tetrarchs, they are harder to identify on the coinage of this period. In general, the iconography of the Tetrarchy may be described as fairly uniform and conservative,[462] in line with a strong military rule, and the coinage is largely consistent with this. The reverse legends GENIO POPVLI ROMANI (on reformed coinage after AD 294) and VIRTVS MILITVM are widely used as is the iconography of Jupiter and Hercules, the deities with which Diocletian and Maximian associated

456 Nixon and Rodgers, 1994, 26.
457 Gillett, 2009, 93.
458 Steinbock, 2014, 51-60; see also Christol, 1976, 421-434.
459 Norena, 2001, 147.
460 Zosimus, *Historia Nova*, Book 2. 7.
461 Nixon and Rodgers, 1994, 193.
462 Rees, 1993, 188.

themselves. Of the nine mints across the Empire that struck for Diocletian and Maximian, the most prolific were Lugdunum, Rome and Antioch.[463] There appears to be a Golden Age basis for a rare issue of coins from Lugdunum struck in AD 293 or 294. Whilst Diocletian's name appears on this coinage, along with Constantius, they appear to have been struck for Maximian at the Lugdunum mint.

It has been observed that Lugdunum issued coins of unusual significance and linked to imperial actions.[464] At the end of AD 293 Maximian and Constantius issued coins from this mint with the reverse inscription SAECVLI FELICITAS (Figure101) which appear to have heralded the theme of the *saeculares* coins of the following year.[465]

In AD 294 the Lugdunum mint struck a series of rare coins which included the reverse inscriptions ROMAE AETERNAE, AETERNITAS AVGG and SAECVLARES AVGG. This group of inscriptions is similar to the Saecular Games coinage of Philip 1 (see Chapter 2.2) and even depict an elephant with a mahout as Philip I had done (Figure 44).

The most significant coins in this group are those with the reverse inscription SAECVLARES AVGG with a dated *cippus*. These coins are issued in the name of Diocletian (Bastien 215), Maximian (Bastien 216) and Constantius (Bastien 217). In each case the *cippus* is inscribed COS X and in the exergue for Diocletian and Maximian is inscribed M XX. Also included in this group are coins issued in the name of Diocletian and Maximian with a reverse inscription of VOT X MXX.

The coins were issued in Lyons in AD 285-294[466] and are very rare indeed. A few of these coins were found in very small numbers in the Lancié hoard.[467] The coins are as follows:

Photo Ref	Bastien ref	Obverse	Reverse	Exergue	Reference
669a	214	CONSTANTIVS NOB C	ROMAE AETERNAE	B	Cohen 258 RIC V 638
669b	214	CONSTANTIVS NOB C	ROMAE AETERNAE	B	Cohen 258
670	217	CONSTANTIVS NOB C	SAECVLARES AVGG	M	Lancié Pl 12
673	216	MAXIMIANVS PF AVG	SAECVLARES AVGG	MXX	Cohen 507

463 Webb, 1929, 194.
464 Steinbock, 2014, 51 -60.
465 Bastien, 1959, 82.
466 Bastien,1972, 254.
467 Lépaulle, 1883, 25.

674	217	CONSTANTIVS NOB C	SAECVLARES AVGG	M	Lancié Pl 12
675	215	DIOCLETIANVS PF AVG	SAECVLARES AVGG	MXX	Lancié Pl 5
676	216	MAXIMIANVS PF AVG	SAECVLARES AVGG	MXX	Cohen 507
677a	221	DIOCLETIANVS PF AVG	VOT X MXX		RIC V 108

Table III: SAECULARES coins issued by the Tetrarchs in Lugdunum

In the Vienna Kunsthistorisches Museum are two of these coins (Figures 68 and 69), for Diocletian and Maximian, each with the *cippus* and the reverse inscription SAECVLARES AVGG and MXX in the exergue.[468]

Figure 68: Radiate of Diocletian (RIC V 78) ©Vienna Kunsthistorisches Museum: RÖ 23975

Figure 69 : Radiate of Maximian (RIC V 415) © Vienna Kunsthistorisches Museum: RÖ 67266

The only coins with the reverse inscription ROMAE AETERNAE (Bastien 669a and 669b above) seem to have been issued in the name of Constantius. Together with the Aeternitas and Saeculares coins they have been interpreted

---

468 Another example of RIC V 415 appeared for sale in 2012: Gemini Auction IX, lot 520, January 2012.

as part of the issue dedicated to the *Saeculares* and the decennial accession of Diocletian.[469]

Also part of this issue were coins which have a forward facing portrait of Maximian and a reverse inscription SAECVLARES AVGG. The reverse design shows an elephant with mahout, which copies the Saecular Games issues of Philip I. Figure 70 shows a *denarius*, but *quinarii* were also issued with the same design.[470]

Figure 70: Denarius of Maximian (Bastien Den 228) © British Museum: 1869 1207 2

The S*aeculares* coins from Lugdunum are not of good quality and appear to have been produced in a hurry. Possibly they were the last coins to be produced by an *officina* in Lugdunum before it was moved to Trier.[471]

AD 294 was a significant year for the newly formed Tetrarchy.[472] It marked the 10th anniversary of Diocletian's reign and in the previous year the usurper Carausius had been killed.[473] There is even a possibility that this coinage represents a re-assertion by the Tetrarchs of a key message employed by the usurper Carausius. These rare Tetrarchic coins indicate that the Golden Age myth and the concept of the *saeculum* may have been used to mark a significant milestone in the rule of the Tetrarchs.

The Arras Medallion

The recovery of Britain by Constantius Chlorus in AD 296 was a major success for the Tetrarchy. A triumphal arch, the *Arcus novus*, was erected in Rome to celebrate the recovery of Britain from the usurpers Carausius and Allectus after ten years.[474] A spectacular gold medallion from the Arras hoard, which is unique, depicts Constantius being greeted by the grateful figure of Londinium gazing up at him (Figure 71). It is thought the hoard of which the medallion was

469 Bastien, 1959, 75-111; Estiot and Zanchi, 2014, 261.

470 Bastien, 1982, 67-70; these coins may have been minted for distribution as ceremonial largesse.

471 Estiot & Zanchi, 2014, 247-296.

472 Bastien, 1959, 75-111.

473 Eutropius, Book 9, 22.

474 Hedlund, 2008, 135.

a part may have belonged to a senior officer who served with Constantius.[475] The reverse inscription reads REDDITOR LVCIS AETERNAE (restorer of the eternal light). The medallion bears the mintmark of Trier.

Figure 71: Electrotype of Medallion of Constantius (RIC VI 34) © British Museum reference: B.11477

The inscription on the medallion recalls the panegyric to Constantius,[476] which celebrates the successful restoration of Britain to the empire in AD 296. The panegyric talks of the Britons who are: *"at last restored to life by the true light of empire".*[477] This phrase, in turn, has echoes of a phrase in Horace who, in an Ode addressed to Augustus, says: *"noble leader bring back light to your country".*[478]

The same passage of this panegyric contains these words: *"Britons exultant with joy came forward with their wives and children venerating you .... whom they gazed at as one who descended from heaven."* [479] This phrase echoes the line in Virgil's Fourth *Eclogue "now is a new race sent down from heaven above."* [480] The panegyrics' use of Golden Age imagery and their link to Tetrarchic coinage has been established.[481] A case can also be made for the Arras medallion of Constantius Chlorus to have allusions not only to Augustus but also to the Augustan Golden Age.

475 Bastien and Metzger, 1977, 215.

476 Toynbee, 1934, 65, note 3; see also the links made in MacCormack,1972,728.

477 *"tandem vera imperii luce recreati";* Panegyric VIII of Constantius, 19.3. Nixon and Rodgers, 1994, 140; see also the reference to Britain being raised to the vision of Roman light *"In conspectum Romane lucis"* Panegyric IX 18.3 – Nixon and Rodgers,1994,169.

478 *"Lucem redde tuae, dux bone, patriae";* Horace, Odes Book IV, V, 5 (translation by G. Barker).

479 *"Exultantesque Britanni cum coniugibus ac liberis obtulerunt .. te ipsum ...quem ut caelo delapsum intuebantur, ... venerantes";* Panegyric VIII Constantius 19.1; Nixon and Rodgers, 1994, 140.

480 *"Iam nova progenies caelo demittitur alto";* Virgil, *Eclogue* IV, 7; See Appendix I.

481 Christol, 1976, 421-434; Moorhead and Stuttard, 2012, 181.

Summary

For the Roman Empire, the third century AD closes with the successful rule of what has come to be known as the Tetrarchy, led by Diocletian and Maximian as joint Augusti. The Tetrarchs were, first and foremost, military men. Yet the written sources continue to include Golden Age allusions and the panegyrics, in particular, make frequent use of Virgilian references which hark back to the Augustan Golden Age.

The coinage of the Tetrarchs mainly employed standardised images and inscriptions with few, if any, references to the Golden Age myth. Yet rare coinage was produced which may allude to Golden Age themes. The rarity indicates it was intended for a small circle of people around the imperial rulers in the western empire; rather in the same way that the panegyrics were intended for an educated elite at the imperial Court. The coinage from the mint at Lugdunum, in particular, has been closely linked with imperial policy, and included a range of designs which can be linked to legitimisation of power through reference to a new *saeculum* and an associated Golden Age.

From the years AD 286 – 293, the usurper emperor Carausius appears to have made extensive use of the Augustan Golden Age myth on his coinage in Britain as part of his claim for legitimisation (see Chapter 6). When Britain was restored to the central empire, the Arras medallion of Constantius Chlorus may also have been intended to allude to the Augustan Golden Age myth.

The mint at Lugdunum produced the incredibly rare SAECVLARES AVGG coinage with the design of a dated *cippus*. It is likely that Zosimus was correct when he recorded the fact that the Saecular Games were not held in Rome under the Tetrarchy.[482] The dated *cippus* coinage, however, along with references in the panegyrics and Zosimus, indicates the interest of Maximian and his court in the Saecular Games and the themes of the Augustan Golden Age myth.

482 Zosimus, *Historia Nova*, Book 2. 7.

4

THE ICONOGRAPHY OF THIRD CENTURY AD COINAGE WITH THE REVERSE INSCRIPTION SAECVLI FELICITAS

The iconography of coinage with the inscription SAECVLI FELICITAS before the third century AD

Felicitas (attracting good fortune as a leader) became a standard quality of ideal military leadership in the republic and was claimed, amongst others, by Sulla and Pompey.[483] The definition is not straightforward and originally implied greatness and glory associated with divine inspiration.[484] Under Augustus it became an imperial attribute but "did not ossify into a static and empty slogan".[485] The term evolved and broadened to become part of the phrase *saeculi felicitas* (good fortune of the *saeculum*). The well-known inscription on an altar from Narbo, dating from the early first century AD, refers to the birthday of Augustus in these terms:

> *"The day when the good fortune of the age brought him forth as the ruler of the world."* [486]

While the phrase does not appear on Augustan coinage, it soon came into more frequent use;[487] in the works of Ovid for example, can be found the phrase *felicia saeculi* (good fortune of the *saeculum*).[488] *Saeculum* can be used in a generic sense of an age or period of time or it can be more specifically interpreted as a Golden Age reference when in a Saecular Games or Golden Age context.

The complex and multiple use of *felicitas* in Roman Imperial times has been well documented.[489] Sometimes the phrase was adapted to *felicitas temporum* or *laetitia temporum* (the joyfulness of the age) and *laetitia* (joy) is closely

---

483 Beard, North, Price, 1998, 219; Luke, 2014,86; for Marius' *Felicitas* see Luke, 2014, 37.
484 Cicero, *De Imperio*, 47.
485 Norena, 2011, 167.
486 *"Qua die eum saeculi felicitas orbi terrarium rectorem edidit"*; CIL XII 4333.
487 Galinsky, 1996, 118.
488 Ovid, Tristia. 1.2.104.
489 Norena, 2011, 165 – 174.

related to *felicitas*.[490] Coins with these adapted inscriptions will be covered in this chapter only if there is a specific Saecular Games or Golden Age reference in the design.[491] On coinage in the second century AD, the phrase SAECVLI FELICITAS was abbreviated to FELIC SAEC as on this *denarius* of Antoninus Pius (Figure 72). The design shows Felicitas holding a short *caduceus* in one hand and leaning on a column.

Figure 72: Denarius of Antoninus Pius (RIC III 309) © British Museum: R.13350

Faustina II issued coinage with the reverse inscription SAECVLI FELICIT with a design of two children on a draped throne or *sella* (Figure 73). In a Golden Age context this may represent the fecundity of the Empress as part of the abundance of the new age. On the gold coins of this design (RIC 709) there are two stars over the heads of the children who may therefore represent the Dioscuri with their appropriate link to divine rebirth (Aeneid, VI, 119-123). There are also implications of the dynastic stability of a new age and the two children may also refer to the birth of twin sons, Commodus and Antoninus, born in AD 161. [492]

Figure 73: Sestertius of Faustina II (RIC III 1665) © British Museum: R.14319

490 Norena, 2011, 172.
491 Strack, 1933, 183; Toynbee, 1986, 90; see Figure 23.
492 Levick, 2014, 115; Yarrow, 2012, 437.

As Commodus proclaimed a new Golden Age at the end of reign,[493] it is not surprising that he too used this phrase on this coin which celebrates his *Decennalia* (Figure 74). Here Victory inscribes a shield mounted on a palm tree.

Figure 74: Denarius of Commodus (RIC III 113) © *British Museum: R.14182*

This Chapter presents a summary survey of the iconography that is used with the reverse inscription SAECVLI FELICITAS and its variations, across the third century AD.

The iconography of the SAECVLI FELICITAS coinage of the Severan dynasty

In the context of an emperor who had celebrated the Saecular Games, the inscription SAECVLI FELICITAS can be directly related to the promise of a new Golden Age brought about by the sacred rituals. The word *Felicitas* appears four times in the surviving parts of the Severan inscription recording the Games.[494] The coinage of the Severan dynasty firmly established the use of the phrase SAECVLI FELICITAS in a Golden Age context[495] and it continued to appear on coinage throughout the third century.

Early on in his reign, Septimius Severus and Julia Domna issued coinage (ascribed to a Syrian mint) with a reverse featuring the inscription SAECVL FELICIT and a design of a crescent moon and seven stars (Figure 75).[496] This design probably refers to the arrival of a new age in an astrological context[497] and follows a coin design used by Hadrian identified as a Golden Age reference.[498] Similar coinage had also been issued by Pescennius Niger[499] and Clodius Albinus[500] the other rivals for the purple at the end of the second century AD.

493 Cassius Dio, LXXI, 15; Hekster, 2002, 98.

494 Pighi, 1941, 141 (line 11), 143 (lines 26, 27 and 34).

495 See Figures 26 and 77.

496 The same reverse inscription appeared on coins with an image of *Felicitas*, with her foot on the prow of a ship and holding cornucopia and *caduceus* RIC V 561.

497 Williams, 2003, 21; Taylor, 1931, 91.

498 E.g. Denarius of Hadrian (RIC 2 part 3, 2019, No 852) see Abdy, 2019, 39; and Strack, 1933,105.

499 RIC IV 73a.

500 RIC IV 38, 49.

Figure 75: Denarius of Septimius Severus (RIC IV 417) © British Museum: 1947,1001.13

Early in the third century, the Rome mint started issuing gold coinage with the reverse inscription FELICITAS SAECVLI, where the second word is inscribed in the exergue (Figure 76). The obverse has a conventional head of Septimius Severus and reverse depicted Julia Domna flanked by her two sons.

Figure 76: Aureus of Septimius Severus (RIC IV 181) © British Museum: R.12666

As Septimius Severus claimed descent from the Antonines,[501] with many coin issues for Julia Domna closely modelled on Faustina I and II (Figure 137), this coin may derive partly from the Faustina II coin illustrated above (Figure 73). It is strikingly similar to a silver coin issued by Augustus with a reverse showing Julia and her two sons Gaius and Lucius.[502] The design can be interpreted as a statement of continuity with dynastic succession as well as the blessings and bounty of a new Golden Age. While these Severan coins pre-date the Saecular Games of AD 204, they can be seen as part of a planned imperial programme of legitimation for the new dynasty amongst the Court elite.[503] The Saecular Games would be the pivotal event to underscore the new Augustan Golden Age.

A similar coin was issued by Septimius Severus at Laodicea with the same reverse inscription but featuring only his two sons Caracalla and Geta (Figure 77).

---

501   See Chapter 2.1.
502   RIC 1 405.
503   Langford, 2013, 19.

Figure 77: Aureus of Septimius Severus (RIC IV 513) © Numismatica Ars
Classica - Auction 49, Lot 309

Julia Domna's key role in establishing the Severan dynasty has been
discussed in chapter 2. Figure 78 shows a coin of Julia Domna with a reverse
image which has been interpreted as Isis.[504] Beneath the inscription SAECVLI
FELICITAS the reverse shows a female figure who holds a baby and has one
foot on a ship's prow.

Figure 78: Aureus of Julia Domna (RIC IV 577) © British Museum: 1896,0608.42

First and foremost, the design makes reference to the fecundity of the
empress and the continuation of the Severan dynasty.[505] The coinage was issued
as aurei, denarii and sestertii from Laodicea and Rome.[506] The reverse image
may be a conflation of Fortuna and Isis.[507] Isis was also the goddess of the sea
and navigation.[508] The navigium isidis was a festival which marked the start
of the seafaring season. [509] The coin image may therefore relate to the arrival
of grain from Egypt, thus linking it to the bountiful nature of the new age. As
a further layer of possible meaning, the worship of Isis is not only connected

504 Mattingly and Sydenham, 1936, 170.
505 Turcan, 1996, 93; see Chapter 5.1 for Julia Domna's coins with the inscription FECVNDITAS.
506 RIC IV 577 645, 865.
507 Rowan, 2011, 252; though statues of Isis Fortuna generally show her holding a cornucopia rather
than a baby e.g. British Museum: 1867.0508.761 (described as Isis Tyche). See introduction.
508 Beresford, 1972, 40.
509 Apuleius, Metamorphoses, 11.5.

with astrology but also with rebirth and cyclical renewal.[510] The development of the mythology which attaches to Isis and Horus is too complex to explore here but it may suffice to quote Apuleius who refers to Isis as *saeculorum progenies initialis* (firstborn of the ages).[511]

In the reign of her son, Caracalla, there is a further example of Julia Domna issuing coinage with the reverse inscription SAECVLI FELICITAS. This time, the reverse type shows a figure of Felicitas sacrificing (Figure 79). Whilst continuing the message of the blessings of a new *saeculum*, the design also emphasises the sacred nature of the Golden Age.

Figure 79: Sestertius of Julia Domna (RIC IV 590) © CNG ref: 943729

In the reign of Elagabalus (AD 218 -22) it seems to have been the senior women at court who took the opportunity to proclaim the continuation of the Severan blessings of the new Golden Age on coinage. Julia Maesa, for example, issued the *denarius*, minted at Rome (Figure 80). An astrological influence may be represented by the star in the right field. This issue was one of the major issues of Maesa's coinage. [512]

Figure 80: Denarius of Julia Maesa (RIC IV 271) © CNG Sale: Nomos 7, Lot: 181 14 May 2014

510   Turcan, 1996, 122.
511   Apuleius, *Metamorphoses*, XI.5.
512   Rowan, 2011, 265.

Whilst coins with SAECVLI FELICITAS generally form less than 1% of coin hoards, the Réka Devnia hoard records 27% of Julia Maesa's coins with this inscription. [513]

The last of the Severan dynasty was Alexander Severus (AD 222-235) who issued coins with this reverse inscription from Antioch (Figure 81).

Figure 81: Denarius of Alexander Severus (RIC IV 299) © British Museum: 1992,0509.189

Orbiana, the wife of Alexander Severus, also issued rare coins with this reverse design (Figure 82).

Figure 82:Denarius of Orbiana (RIC IV 325) © British Museum: 1992,0509.189

SAECVLI FELICITAS coinage of Gordian III

Following the end of the Severan dynasty in AD 235, there was a rapid succession of short-lived emperors until Gordian III assumed the purple in AD 238. Towards the end of his reign, Gordian III issued SAECVLI FELICITAS coins as part of the second series of radiates issued in Antioch from AD 242-244 (Figure 83). [514] Of the twelve reverse types issued in the second series, three were produced in substantially higher quantities than any of the others. These comprised: FORTVNA REDVX, ORIENS AVG and SAECVLI FELICITAS. It has been estimated that these were approximately ten times as common as the other types, with over 640 known specimens of SAECVLI FELICITAS reverse

513 Mouchmov, 1934, 128 (316 coins in a total of 1141 for Julia Maesa).
514 Bland, 1991, 218.

types alone. Of the 8,890 coins of Gordian III in the Dorchester Hoard, 1.7% were of this type.

Figure 83: Radiate of Gordian III (RIC IV 216) © British Museum: 1937,0406.613

The spear may represent world and military domination and the globe may represent the cosmos[515] - an appropriate image for association with a new *saeculum*. It is possible that Gordian III may have been preparing for the millennial Saecular Games[516] and this issue was advance notice of a new Golden Age.

SAECVLI FELICITAS coinage of Trajan Decius and Trebonianus Gallus

Trajan Decius ruled from AD 249-251 and issued a new type of coin – the double *sestertius* – with the words of the familiar phrase reversed i.e. FELICITAS SAECVLI (Figure 84). The design shows Felicitas holding a long *caduceus* and cornucopia.

Figure 84: Double Sestertius of Trajan Decius (RIC IV 115c) © British Museum: 1867,0101.2142

515 Hijmans, 2009, 75; Hedlund, 2008, 225-226.
516 The animals which appeared in Philip's Saecular Games may have been assembled by Gordian III: *SHA* 20,33.

Trajan Decius claimed a new Golden Age by issuing coins with NOVVM SAECVLVM (Figure 49) in the name of his son and his wife. To issue a new type of coin, which weighed over 30 grams, was a significant statement. It follows that the reverse inscription was also linked to the claim of a new Golden Age.

Trebonianus Gallus also issued a medallion with the inscription SAECVLI FELICITAS with an image of the four seasons (Figure 126).[517]

FELICITAS SAECVLI coinage of Valerian and Gallienus

The next recorded use of FELICITAS SAECVLI on coinage appears in the reign of Valerian (AD 253-260). Firstly, the legend appears on rare coins minted in Antioch with an image of Diana Lucifera (Figure 85). His son Gallienus (AD 253-268) also produced rare coins with the same design.[518] See Chapter 3.1 for links between Diana and the Golden Age.

Figure 85: Radiate of Valerian (RIC V 213) © Gorny & Mosch sale 212, Lot 2971 March 2013

At about the same time, from the same mint, coins were struck which depicted Saturn (Figure 56) which also links to a new Golden Age.[519]

Valerian[520] and Gallienus (Figure 86) issued equally rare coins with the inscription SAECVLI FELICITAS from a mint in Europe (possibly Viminacium). The design shows Felicitas holding a long *caduceus* and cornucopia.

Figure 86: Radiate of Gallienus (RIC V 249var) © Roma Numismatics E-sale 3 Lot 717 Nov. 2013

---

517 Cohen, 1880, Trebonianus Gallus No. 109, 250; Toynbee, 1986, 90.

518 RIC V 291 (var): Gallienus SAECVLI FELICITAS with Diana Lucifer.

519 See Introduction and Chapter 3.1.

520 RIC V 249: Valerian SAECVLI FELICITAS.

SAECVLI FELICITAS coinage of the Gallic Empire

After he became sole ruler, Gallienus faced several usurpations including that of Postumus in northern Europe.[521] The so-called 'Gallic Empire' lasted from AD 260 to AD 274 when Tetricus was defeated by Aurelian. The coinage of the 'Gallic Empire', which often copied designs of earlier emperors, included the reverse inscription SAECVLI FELICITAS which can be seen to lay claim to a Golden Age[522] as an act of legitimation by usurper emperors.[523]

Figure 87: Radiate of Postumus (RIC V 83)   Mairat,365   © CNG reference: 160294

The coins of Postumus with this inscription are from Trier and featured the emperor holding a globe and spear (Figure 87) following the design of Gordian III (Figure 80 above). 330 examples of this coin have been recorded.[524]

Figure 88: Aureus of Marius (RIC V 10) Mairat, 537-8 © CNG reference: 786461

Marius, who also issued his coins from Trier, chose to depict Felicitas with caduceus and cornucopia (Figure 88). Only one example of the aureus is known, whilst the radiates with this inscription comprise nearly 50% of all the known coins from issue 2 at Trier in AD 269. [525]

---

521 Aurelius Victor, 33; see Potter, 2004, 260.

522 Manders, 2012, 307; Christol, 1987, 10.

523 See discussion on Postumus Chapter 3.1; see Chapter 6 on Carausius.

524 Mairat, 2014, 323.

525 Mairat, 2014 pp340 -341.

A more striking image with this phrase is provided by Victorinus who chose to depict Isis[526] on his coinage which was also minted at Trier (Figure 89). Six examples of *aurei* with this inscription are known. [527]

Figure 89: Aureus of Victorinus (RIC V 100) Mairat, 614-6 © British Museum: 1850,0601.19

This coin appears to copy a design of Julia Domna (Figure 78) with the same inscription. Victorinus also issued *denarii* from Cologne with this inscription, with a design similar to that of Postumus above.[528] Tetricus reverts to a more standard image of Felicitas with cornucopia; though here the design has been adapted to show Felicitas sacrificing at an altar (Figure 90). Four examples are known. [529]

Figure 90: Radiate of Tetricus (RIC V 22) Mairat 828 © British Museum 1962,1212.86

---

526 Or Isis/ Fortuna see discussion at Figure 78.
527 Mairat, 2014, 346.
528 Mairat, 2014 353 (one example known from Frome).
529 Mairat, 2014, 366.

The SAECVLI FELICITAS coinage from Claudius Gothicus to Carinus

The reverse inscription SAECVLI FELICITAS appears on coinage in the reigns of Claudius Gothicus (AD 268-270) and Quintillus (AD 270)[530] as on this Radiate of Claudius Gothicus (Figure 91).

Figure 91: Radiate of Claudius Gothicus (RIC V I 179 var) © Wildwinds image

Aurelian (AD 270-275) issued coins with the inscription FELIC SAECVLI minted in Milan (Figure 92).

Figure 92: Radiate of Aurelian (RIC V 112) © British Museum: 1962,1212.86

Aurelian also issued coins with the inscription SAECVLI FELICITAS from Siscia.[531] The inscription RESTIT SAECVLI (restorer of the age) also appears on coins from Siscia, where the emperor is shown receiving a wreath from a female figure (Figure 93). This reverse design is also seen on coins with the reverse inscription RESTITVTOR ORBIS (restorer of the world).[532]

Figure 93: Radiate of Aurelian (RIC V 235 var) © Wildwinds image

530 RIC V 1 30 and 39.
531 RIC V 352.
532 RIC V 1 290.

With the defeat of Zenobia in the east and Tetricus in the west, Aurelian could rightly lay claim to be the restorer of the Roman world (*restitutor orbis*).[533] Aurelian developed a particular affinity for Sol, partly perhaps as a legacy from Gallienus and partly as a link to solar cults in the eastern empire.[534] The combination of solar imagery and use of the phrases SAECVLI FELICITAS and RESTITVTOR SAECVLI may be seen to add a cosmic aspect to his success.

The short-lived reigns of the emperors Tacitus (AD 275-276) and Florian (AD 276) both saw coins issued with this inscription. For Tacitus, the coin (Figure 94) was part of series which emphasised the peace of a Golden Age which the emperor would bring about through his *virtus* (military excellence).[535] A similar range of coins were issued by Florian in conjunction with that illustrated at Figure 95. It has been noted that on the coinage of Florian "the assurances of a new *aurea aetas* are even more insistent".[536]

Figure 94: Radiate of Tacitus (Estiot 2201) © *Wildwinds image*

Figure 95: Radiate of Florian (RIC V 62) © *Numismatik Naumann Auction March 2013 Lot 264*

In many respects, Probus can be seen to be carrying on the work of Aurelian,[537] and his coinage carries many of the same inscriptions, including

533 Potter, 2004, 272.

534 Watson,1999, 189.

535 Hedlund, 2008, 82. For *virtus* and the Golden Age see discussion in Chapter 6.

536 Hedlund, 2008, 82. Reverse inscriptions include VIRTVS FLORIANI AVG.

537 Southern, 2015, 187.

FELICITAS SAECVLI, also abbreviated to FELICITAS SEC (Figure 96). These coins were issued by mints at Ticinum and Siscia. Probus also issued medallions with the inscription SAECVLI FELICITAS.[538]

Figure 96: Radiate of Probus (RIC V 359) © CNG reference 804364

The coinage of Probus repeatedly emphasises the *securitas* (security) of the empire.[539] Issued at the same time as the FELICITAS SAECVLI issues are *aurei* minted at Siscia with the reverse SECVRITAS SAECVLI (security of the age), which may serve to emphasise the security brought about by a new age (Figure 97).

Figure 97: Aureus of Probus (RIC V 593) © British Museum: 1860,0329.18

The Caran dynasty (AD 282 – 285) issued coins with the reverse inscription such as this Radiate of Carus and Carinus (Figure 98). Portraying father and son has dynastic overtones of a new age. The reverse design repeats the image of the emperor holding globe and spear. Carinus also issued coins with this reverse in his own name.[540]

---

538 Gnecchi, II 119, 37.
539 Hedlund, 2008, 83; A bronze test strike of an *aureus* of Probus from Siscia with the reverse inscription FELICITAS SAECVLI is held in a Swiss private collection. There are three figures on the reverse: the emperor, Felicitas and a togate male.
540 RIC V 2 152.

Figure 98: Radiate of Carus and Carinus (RIC V 2 141) © Numismatica Ars Classica Auction 72, Lot 742, May 2013

SAECVLI FELICITAS coinage of the 'British Empire'

Given that Carausius issued so many coins with Golden Age iconography (see Chapter 6), it is not perhaps surprising that he too issued coins with the reverse inscription SAECVLI FELICITA(S) (Figure 99). The reverse design shows the emperor holding globe and spear as on the coins of Gordian III, Postumus and Carinus. The mint mark is CXXI and indicates this was an issue early in the reign, once Carausius had established the C mint in Britain.[541]

Figure 99: Radiate of Carausius (RIC V 395) © British Museum: 1925,0316.362

Carausius also issued coins with the reverse inscription RESTIT SAECVL (restoration of the ages).[542] which may be linked to the restoration of the Golden Age *saeculum*.

Although Allectus did not issue the range of coinage with Golden Age allusions, as Carausius did, he nonetheless issued coins with the reverse legend FELICITAS SEC, like Probus, with the figure of Felicitas with *caduceus* and cornucopia (Figure 100).

---

541 Moorhead, RIC forthcoming.
542 RIC V II 384- 386.

Figure 100: Radiate of Allectus (RIC V 18) © British Museum: 1929,0706.10

SAECVLI FELICITAS coinage of the Tetrarchy

As mentioned in Chapter 3.2, Maximian issued coins from Lugdunum with the reverse inscription SAECVLI FELICITAS (Figure 101). The design is that of Felicitas leaning on a low column with her right hand raised to her head. The coin is similar to the image on the coins of Antoninus Pius (Figure 72). The design also recalls earlier coins depicting Securitas[543] and may have been intended to convey the sense of security brought about by a new age. This issue in around AD 293 appears to be a precursor to the SAECVLARES issue from the same mint.[544] This design was also issued in the name of Constantius from the same mint.[545]

Figure 101: Radiate of Maximian (RIC V 416) © Paul Francis Jacquier auction 39 Lot 666 September 2014

Perhaps the most extraordinary example of the use of SAECVLI FELICITAS is on a lead test strike for a medallion probably issued in Gaul in the reign of Diocletian (Figure 102). [546]

---

543 E.g. Probus RIC V 525.

544 Bastien, 1959, 82.

545 RIC V 640.

546 Bastien, Amandry, Gautier, 1989, 9.

Figure 102: Medallion from Lyon - drawing by Encina and published in de La Saussaye, "Lettre à M. A. De Longpérier" Revue numismatique. Nouvelle Série 7 (1862) 426-431

The upper register depicts two seated, nimbate emperors who may be Diocletian and Maximian[547] though they have also been interpreted as Maximian and Constantius.[548] Behind them stand two soldiers. In front of the emperors is a crowd of adulatory men, women and children who may be receiving bounty from the emperors or, more probably, they are paying homage to the semi-divine emperors. The lower register pictures a *castellum* or fortified city named as Mogantiacum, with the river Rhine also named.

Apart from identifying the city, the interpretation of the iconography is not straightforward. Possible links with the Panegyric of Constantius have been made,[549] but there may be a more specific link with the Panegyric of Eumenius. This Panegyric contains a specific reference to Golden Age and relates it to the age of Saturn.[550] Immediately preceding this reference is this passage:

> *"Why should I count up the camps of cavalry units and cohorts re-established all along the Rhine, Danube and Euphrates frontiers? How many trees set out by hand grow strong in the mild weather of spring or fall, how many crops, once beaten by the rain, rise up again in the heat*

547 Bastien, Amandry, Gautier, 1989, 15.
548 Alföldi, 1958, 67-68; see note 28 in Nixon and Rodgers, 1994, 121.
549 Bastien, Amandry, Gautier, 1989, 10.
550 See discussion at Figure 56 in Chapter 3.1.

of summer, as walls, the traces of their old foundations discernible, which are being erected everywhere." [551]

This passage refers specifically to the Rhine, to the re-establishment of army units and, above all to the building of walls. The link between the Augustan Golden Age and walls is made clear in the *Aeneid*,[552] as Saturn was not only an agricultural deity but one who founded the walls of Rome.[553] The Panegyric of Eumenius is addressed to Maximian but contains references to all four Tetrarchs and the recovery of Britain. Therefore, it must be dated after AD 296. The likely date is between AD 297-299.[554] It is appropriate that the medallion, with its visual emphasis on fortified walls, pictures the two senior Augusti. The Panegyric of Eumenius refers to the Golden Age being under the auspices of Jupiter and Hercules, the presiding deities of Diocletian and Maximian.

From these links, it is possible to interpret the iconography of this medallion as part of the Golden Age imagery, particularly with the inscription SAECVLI FELICITAS. If so, the links between the panegyrics and the numismatic issues of the Tetrarchy [555] are strengthened even further.

Summary

SAECVLI FELICITAS on coinage is sometimes seen as a phrase that became something of a trope in the third century AD. [556] Nevertheless, claims of a new Golden Age can be associated with the emperors who issued coins with this inscription. The hoard data available indicate these were usually not common coins and, in most cases, they probably represent less than 1% of the coinage of the relevant emperor.

The Severan dynasty employed the inscription SAECVLI FELICITAS on coinage which had iconography related to the promise of a new Golden Age brought about by the Saecular Games. Some coin designs highlight the new dynasty by including portraits of the sons Caracalla and Geta. Other images show Felicitas sacrificing which may have emphasised the sacred nature of the new age.

The image on the coins of Gordian III with this inscription, show the young emperor advancing with spear and globe. These attributes may represent power over the earth and the cosmos. It is possible that Gordian III issued these coins

---

551 *"Nam quid ego alarum et cohortium castra percenseam toto Rheni et Histri at Eufrate limite restitua? Qua veris autumniue clementia tot manu positae arbores convalescunt, quo calore solis tot depressae imbribus segetes resurgunt, quot ubique muri vix repertis veterum funamentorum vestigiis excitantur"*. Eumenius, Panegyric IX, 18.4; Nixon and Rodgers, 1994, 169-170.

552 Virgil, *Aeneid*, VIII, 355-358.

553 Scully,1988, 69-78.

554 Nixon and Rodgers, 1994, 148.

555 Steinbock, 2014, 51-60.

556 Galinsky, 1996, 118.

as a precursor to arranging the Millennial Games which came to be celebrated by Philip I.

The inscription does not appear on Philip's coinage but then is used to great effect by Trajan Decius on a new denomination, the double *sestertius*. The image on this striking coin is that of Felicitas holding a *caduceus* and cornucopia. Decius also issued coins in the name of his wife and son with the reverse inscription SAECVLVM NOVVM.[557] Therefore, the use of the phrase FELICITAS SAECVLI on a new denomination can be seen to be highlighting the blessings of a new Golden Age.

Valerian and Gallienus depict an image of Diana Lucifera on coins with this inscription as well as the image of Felicitas which appeared on the coins of Trajan Decius. Gallienus issued rare coinage with the reverse inscription SAECVLARES AVG as well as other coinage with Golden Age iconography.[558]

The coinage of the "Gallic Empire" displays a wonderful variety of iconography for coins with this reverse inscription. Indeed, in this period, all the images which appeared on coins prior to that time are reused. Extraordinarily, this includes an image of Isis (or Isis Fortuna) during the reign of Victorinus which had previously appeared on the coins of Julia Domna. While these designs can be seen as mere copies of earlier coins they may equally have been deliberately selected to underscore the need of any usurper to seek legitimation.[559] It is interesting to note that the inscription was important enough to be included on several gold issues.

The use of the inscription on the coinage is continued by the emperors who reigned from AD 268-285 with a variety of the previous images. The claim that each emperor brought about the return of a Golden Age became a "recurrent theme." [560]

The coinage issued by Carausius, Maximian, Diocletian and Contantius with SAECVLI FELICITAS tends to reassert a specific Golden Age message. The design on the rare coinage of Maximian and Constantius issued from Lugdunum depicts Felicitas leaning on a low column with one hand held to her head. Maximian's SAECVLI FELICITAS seems to have been issued as a precursor to the later SAECVLARES coinage, as was that of Carausius.

The inscription makes a final and spectacular appearance on a unique lead test-strike for a medallion issued under the Tetrarchy. There is a good case to be made that the iconography here can be directly linked to Golden Age allusions in the panegyrics.

---

557 Figure 50.

558 See Chapter 3.1.

559 The Gallic Empire also issued coins of unusual design e.g. featuring Apollo and Diana, the deities of the Augustan Golden Age: Mairat, 2014, Postumus 372.

560 Hedlund, 2008, 80.

5

THE ICONOGRAPHY OF TELLUS, AION, THE FOUR SEASONS AND THE PHOENIX ON COINAGE OF THE THIRD CENTURY AD

5.1 The iconography of Tellus

The written sources

Varro listed Tellus among the twelve main Roman agricultural deities.[561] He lists her second only to Jupiter and says that *"Jupiter is called 'the Father', and Tellus is called 'Mother Earth'.* [562] As the female personification of the productive power of the earth,[563] she came to be regarded as an Earth Mother in a role not dissimilar to that of Demeter in the Greek pantheon.[564]

References to Tellus abound in Virgil's works. In the Georgics, Virgil uses the phrase *"Saturnia tellus"* (Saturnian land) in the context of a Golden Age reference.[565]

According to Varro, the first known sacrificial animal was the pig[566] and it is likely that the earliest sacrifices were to agricultural deities which included Tellus.[567] Horace refers to *"Tellurem porco"* (the pig dedicated to Tellus). [568] In Virgil's Georgics, Tellus is frequently combined with the adjective *fecunda* (fruitful).[569]

---

561 Varro, *De Re Rustica,* 1, I, 5; Her temple, said to date from 268 BC, was situated on the Esquiline hill in Rome and she was worshipped in the ancient ritual of *fordicidia* which celebrated the fertility of the earth and flocks: Rantala, 2016, 71-72.

562 *"Iuppiter pater appellatur, Tellus terra mater."*

563 Adkins, 1996, 218.

564 Scullard, 1981, 102.

565 Johnston, 1980, 51; Nappa, 2005, 84.

566 Varro, *De Re Rustica,* II iv 9.

567 Brouwer, 1989, 351.

568 Horace, *Epistulae,* 2 i 143.

569 Virgil, *Georgics* I, l. 67; the phrase also occurs in an inscription from the Mithraeum at Santa Prisca, Rome: Vermaseren and Van Essen, 1965, 187.

Virgil's Fourth *Eclogue*, the key text for the Augustan Golden Age, mentions Tellus both in the sense of the earth and as the name of the goddess.[570] The references to Tellus in the Fourth *Eclogue* may be construed as incorporating references to the goddess Ceres, another agricultural goddess, who was the daughter of Saturn and Ops. While Tellus and Ceres have their own origins and cults, it is perhaps true to say that Tellus and Ceres could be regarded as aspects of the same divine force.[571] Ovid links Tellus and Ceres together:

"Placate Tellus and Ceres, the mothers of fruitfulness, with their own spelt and teeming sow. Ceres and Earth perform a common function: one gives the corn its life force, the other allows its allotted place." [572]

The Sybilline oracle for the Saecular Games, preserved by Zosimus,[573] contains a clear reference to sacrifices for the goddess Tellus as part of the rituals:

"(Those finished) offer a black hog and sow To Tellus, for the product of the plough." [574]

The *Carmen Saeculare* also contains a direct reference to the goddess Tellus which is appropriately linked to Ceres:

"Let Earth (Tellus) that is fruitful in crops, and in cattle, Adorn our Ceres with garlands of wheat-ears." [575]

The surviving inscriptions from the Saecular Games of Augustus and Septimius Severus refer not to Tellus but to Terra Mater.[576] It appears that the older and more traditional deity in Roman religion was Tellus and it may be that employing Terra Mater was part of Augustus's reinterpretation of the Golden Age myth.[577] Terra Mater may be linked to the Greek goddess Demeter and the Eleusinian Mysteries.[578] As discussed in the introduction, while the Augustan inscription contain references to *"Graeco archivo ritu"* (ancient Greek ritual) and Greek deities, in fact the ceremonies were thoroughly Roman.[579] Whilst there must have been a distinction between these goddesses, the practice of

---

570 Virgil, Fourth *Eclogue*, 19,33,39.

571 Whittaker, 2007, 71; Rantala, 2016, 75.

572 *"placentur frugum matres, Tellusque Ceresque, farre suo gravidae visceribusque suis: officium commune Ceres et Terra tuentur; haec praebet causam frugibus, illa locum."* Ovid, *Fasti*, 672-704 (translation by G. Barker).

573 Zosimus, Book 2, 6-7.

574 Zosimus, Book 2, 13-14 (Green and Chaplin).

575 *"fertilis frugum pecorisque Tellus spicea donet Cererem corona"* Horace, Carmen Saeculare, 29-30

576 Pighi, 1941, 116, IV.134 (Augustus) and 162, V.49 (Septimius Severus).

577 Forsyth, 2012, 73; see introduction.

578 Whittaker, 2007, 75.

579 Scheid, 1995, 15-31; cf. Schnegg-Kohler, 2002; Lipka, 2009, 152; see also Ovid *Fasti* 1.657.

conflating deities, together with the numismatic evidence of the second and third centuries, tend to indicate that Terra Mater and Tellus came to be regarded as constituents of the same divine spark. In other words, Terra Mater may have become known by her Roman name of Tellus.[580]

The continuance of the ritual association between Ceres and Tellus into the third century AD is attested by Arnobius (died c AD 330), who was a Christian writer under Diocletian's reign:

> *"The lectisternium of Ceres will be on the next Ides. For the gods have beds and so they can sleep on softer beds, the impression of the cushions is lifted up and it is raised. It is the birthday of Tellus."* [581]

The poem known as *Precatio Terrae* (Prayer to the Earth) was also probably written in the third century AD[582] and this addresses Tellus as *"rerum naturae parens"* (procreator of all things).[583]

The iconography of Tellus on Roman Imperial coinage

Hadrian (AD 117-138) is the first emperor to issue coinage with a reverse inscription TELLVS STABIL on silver[584] and bronze coinage (Figure 103). Tellus reclines on a basket of agricultural produce and one hand rests on a globe. She sits under a vine tree which may indicate the fruitfulness of the earth.[585] In one sense, this coinage declares the agricultural prosperity and stability achieved under Hadrian's rule. TELLVS STABIL therefore can be seen to represent universal peace.[586]

Figure 103: Dupondius of Hadrian (RIC II part 3 2019, No .2178) © British Museum reference: R.9163

580 Rantala, 2013, 98; see also Gesztelyi, 1981, 429 – 456.
581 *"Lectisternium Cereris erit Idibus proximis. Habent enim dii lectos atque ut stratis possint mollioribus incubare, pulvinorum tollitur atque excitatur impressio. Telluris natalis est."* (translation by A. Bryce) Arnobius, *Adversus Nationes*, Lib VII, 32. 8 – 9.
582 Vermaseren, 1965, 188.
583 Wight-Duff, 1934, 342-350.
584 RIC II 277d.
585 See Figures 112/113 and discussion below on the possible symbolism of the vine.
586 Toynbee, 1934, 140.

Given Hadrian's Golden Age imagery on gold coinage (Figure 117) and his identification with Augustus,[587] the link between the Tellus representations with the Golden Age myth can be clearly made.[588] In addition, Tellus was linked to the anniversary of the birth of Roma at this time.[589] Medallions were issued by Hadrian which expanded this design to include the four seasons, [590] a design that was to be revived in the third century. Another image of Tellus appears on Hadrianic coinage where she is standing, holding a plough and a hoe, with two ears of corn at her side (Figure 104).

Figure 104: Denarius of Hadrian (RIC II part 3 2019 No 2052) © British Museum reference: R.12304

Antoninus Pius (AD 138- 161) issued medallions on which Tellus appears (Figure 105). Although the numismatic evidence is scanty, it is thought that Antoninus Pius celebrated the 900th anniversary of the foundation of Rome in around AD 148.[591]

Figure 105: Medallion of Antoninus Pius (Gnecchi, 1912, II p 20/97) © British Museum: 1853,0512.230

---

587 Kristsotakis, 2008, 121; Toynbee, 1986, 140.

588 Rantala 2013, 99; Bellen, 1997, 136.

589 Rantala, 2013, 99; Gesztelyi, 1981, 442.

590 Gnecchi, III 19.90.

591 Levick, 2014, 102; Whetstone,1978, 25.

Here Tellus reclines on a cow while playing about her are the four seasons with zodiacal signs. The association of Tellus and a cow is reminiscent of the "Tellus panel" on the Ara Pacis of Augustus (Figure 106).[592] This famous "mother earth" image has been much discussed and is probably a conflation of several goddesses including Tellus, Pax, Ceres, Ops and possibly Venus.[593]

Figure 106: The "Tellus" panel from the Ara Pacis © 2019 G Barker

The iconography of Tellus on coinage of the third century AD

As discussed in the chapter above, Septimius Severus sought to underpin his legitimacy by claiming descent from Antoninus Pius, amongst others, and portrayed himself as brother to Commodus.[594] Not surprisingly, therefore, Septimius Severus copied coin designs from Commodus to bolster his claim that he brought back a Golden Age.

Tellus first appears on Septimius Severus's coinage on a dated *aureus* minted in Rome in AD 197-198 (Figure 107). Though this is late second century, it has been included here as an important part of the iconography. The design copies the Antoninus Pius medallion at Figure 108, and also appears on coinage of Commodus.[595]

---

592 LIMC, VII, 2 605; further images of Tellus appear in LIMC, VII, 2 605-611.

593 Toynbee, 1934, 140; Spaeth, 1981, 65-100; De Grummond, 1990, 663-677; Galinsky, 1996, 148; Rehak, 2006, 109. A similar panel from Carthage, in the Louvre, indicates the image was replicated in the provinces (NN975 Ma 1838).

594 Cassius Dio,*Historia Romana*, LXXVI. 7.

595 Gnecchi II 52, 3.

Figure 107: Aureus of Septimius Severus (RIC IV 102) © British Museum: 1850,0412.131

Figure 108: Medallion of Antoninus Pius (Gnecchi, 1912, II, p16/67) © British Museum: 1872,0709.377

The coin reverses at Figures 107 and 108 highlight the figure of Sol in his chariot. The importance of Sol in the Augustan Saecular Games has also been seen in the context of his role as legendary ancestor to the Latin people,[596] with the assimilation of the gods of Latium as part of Augustus's deliberate political strategy. The message of imperial expansion was implicit in the Augustan writings[597] and conquering the Latins acted as "a paradigm for Rome's wider empire". [598]

596 Galinsky, 1967, 164.
597 Horace, *Carmen Saeculare*, 53-56: '*iam mari terraque manus potentis Medus Albanasque timet secures iam Scythae responsa petunt, superbi nuper et Indi*' (Now the Parthians fear our forces, powerful on land, and on sea: they fear the Alban axes, Now the once proud Indians, now the Scythians beg for an answer). See Appendix II.
598 Cooley, 2006, 236.

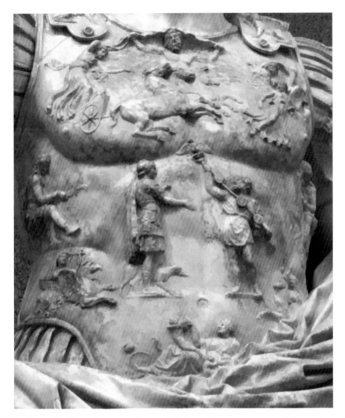

Figure 109: Details from breast plate of Prima Porta statue of Augustus, Musei Vaticani, photo by G Barker

This design, known through very few examples, also brings to mind the Prima Porta statue of Augustus (Figure 109). Elements of this breastplate include Tellus, at the foot of this illustration, and, top left, Sol preceded by Aurora who can be seen as heralding the light of the Golden Age.[599]

Tellus, or Terra Mater, also appears on coins of Septimius Severus (Figure 10) and Caracalla (Figure 110) which seem to be based on a design of the coins of Domitian (Figure 111). While most elements of the design remain the same, Liber Pater and Hercules, the Severan patron deities, have been added on the right side of the scene. The issue in Caracalla's name was probably intended to emphasise Caracalla's role as the heir to the dynasty and the continuation of the promised Golden Age.

599 Galinsky, 1996, 158-159; The image brings to mind the third stanza of Horace's *Carmen Saeculare*: "O kindly sun in your shining chariot, who heralds the day and then hides it to be born again, new yet the same, you will never know anything mightier than Rome" (translation by A Kline); this passage has been described as "one of the most glorious passages in ancient poetry": Fraenkel, 1957, 371. See Appendix II.

Figure 110: Sestertius of Caracalla (RIC IV 418) © British Museum: R.15816

While Tellus is identified by the presence of the sacrificial sow, her usual cornucopia appears to have been replaced by flowing drapery. [600]

Figure 111: Sestertius of Domitian (RIC II i 612) © British Museum: R.11398

The coinage of Julia Domna includes images of Tellus, appropriately combined with the inscription FECVNDITAS (Figure 112). This image, copied from the coinage of Commodus (Figure 113), links to his claim of new Golden Age.

Figure 112: Aureus of Julia Domna (RIC IV 549) © British Museum: 1844,1015.225

---

600 Cf. the coin in the Vienna Kunsthistorisches Museum (RÖ 15392) where the flowing drapery is clearer.

Figure 113: Medallion of Commodus (Gnecchi 1912, II p 65/125) © CNG sale 9, January 2007, Lot 651

In this image, Tellus reclines on a basket of plenty and her hand rests on a globe of the cosmos representing cyclical time. The four seasons, as children,[601] process across the globe to welcome the return of agricultural abundance represented by Tellus. To the left of the scene is a vine tree and this may relate to the passage in *Dionysiaca* by Nonnus which relates the four seasons' visit to Helios to learn about the prophecy of a vine tree. In this prophecy, the cosmic balance embodied in their continuous succession will only be complete when Ampelos is changed into a vine and wine is discovered.[602] Vines may also have been a more general symbol for the fertility of the Golden Age.[603]

Figure 114: Denarius of Julia Domna (RIC IV 549) © British Museum: 1946,1004.830

This image was employed on several denominations issued in Julia Domna's name including *denarii* (Figure 114).[604] Septimius Severus also issued a version of this coin.[605] Julia Domna's FECVNDITAS coinage is more

---

601 See Chapter 5.2.

602 Nonnus, *Dionysiaca*, 12.1 – 192; Miguéulez-Cavero, 2013, 357.

603 Zanker, 1990, 179.

604 E.g. RIC IV 549 and RIC V 783.

605 RIC IV 758.

common than many of the types illustrated here. However, in the Réka Devnia hoard, just seven coins had the reverse inscription of FECVNDITAS with a figure of Tellus from the total of 3,409 recorded for the empress.

Otacilia Severa was later to issue similar coinage from Antioch in Philip I's reign (AD 244-249) although these coins are incredibly rare and only one or two examples are known (Figure 115).[606] The reverse inscription is FECVNDITAS TEMPORVM and, at first sight, the design appears similar to Julia Domna's coin. There are differences, however, as the female reclining figure holds a cornucopia and grain ears and is shown with only two children.[607] The two children may be Romulus and Remus, as Virgil wrote that when the Golden Age returned, Romulus and Remus would be born again as law makers.[608]

Figure 115: Radiate of Otacilia Severa (RIC IV 132) © CNG, Triton Auction, Lot 1610, 1 Dec. 1997

The reclining female may represent Ceres or some other figure of fecundity, though other representations of Tellus also show her with two children as on the Gemma Augustea (Figure 116).[609] She is shown seated, lower right, holding a cornucopia, with her elbow on the throne of Augustus with one child behind and the other in front. Above Augustus is a roundel with his adopted astrological sign, Capricorn and the *sidus Iulium*, both symbols of the Augustan Golden Age.[610]

606 An example is in Bibliotèque National de France, Cabinet des Médailles 7957.
607 Cf the image of Tellus on the Prima Porta cuirass with a crown of wheat, two children and a cornucopia.
608 Virgil, *Aeneid* I, 292- 293.
609 Balbuza, 2014, 189; Toynbee, 1934, 141.
610 Williams, 2003, 24.

Figure 116: Detail from the Gemma Augustea © Kunsthistorisches Museum Vienna

Summary

The inclusion of Tellus in the Augustan Golden Age myth is clear from the references in Virgil's Georgics and the Fourth *Eclogue*. This goddess features in the *Carmen Saeculare* and the surviving Sybilline prophecy. As one of the ancient agricultural deities, her role was to symbolise agricultural fertility with the returning Golden Age.

Tellus appears on the coinage of Septimius Severus which appears to be influenced by Augustan iconography. The Saecular Games coinage of Septimius Severus and Caracalla show Tellus on images of the Saecular Games rituals which are similar to those which appear on the coins of Domitian.

Julia Domna's coinage include images of Tellus with a reverse inscription FECVNDITAS. This combines the Golden Age reference of plenty while proclaiming the fecundity of the Empress and her ability to provide heirs for the emperor. These coins proclaim a new dynasty in the context of a Golden Age. Otacilia Severa issued coins which appear to be based on the Tellus coinage of Julia Domna but this time feature only two children, for which there are precedents in Augustan images.

Coinage from the third century AD with the image of Tellus is rare and, in most cases, represents less than 1% of the coins issued. As previously argued, this would indicate that the images were intended for a small circle with the imperial court as part of the programme of legitimation.

5.2 The iconography of Aion and the four seasons

The written sources

In one sense, Aion can be seen as a representation of eternal time and has been defined as "time in an absolute sense".[611] However, the many references to Aion, in ancient Greek literature alone, need careful analysis and qualification.[612] References to Aion can be found, for example, in the *Iliad* [613] where the word equates to life or lifetime and in Plato[614] who contrasts Aion as ideal eternity with Chronos, or empirical time.

The concept of Aion becomes even more complex at the time of Ptolemaic Egypt and then develops further in the Roman imperial period.[615] At Alexandria, Aion may have been identified with Serapis and with the rebirth of Osiris.[616] At some stage Dionysus was identified with Aion in terms of a god that was repeatedly reborn.[617]

In the second and third centuries AD, the so-called mystery cults, including those of Cybele, Isis and Serapis, experienced a growth in popularity.[618] The cult of Mithras, with its roots in Persia, became particularly popular in military circles. Mithraism appears to have had a fundamental root in astrology and a belief in cyclical time.[619]

The interpretations of Aion multiply greatly in the third century AD.[620] In The *Enneads*, a major Neoplatonist work by Plotinus (AD 204-270), the title of one of the tracts is : Περὶ αἰῶνος καὶ χρόνου (On time and eternity) in which Aion appears.[621] Statues of lion-headed men wrapped in the coils of a snake, found in Mithraea, are often interpreted as Aion (or Phanes) who may have been equated with Saturn;[622] though any such interpretation remains hypothetical.

In *Dionysiaca* by Nonnus (4th[th]/5th[th] century AD), Aion is a central figure who represents eternal or cyclical time.[623] Aion appears as a youthful or as an

611 Levi, 1944, 274.
612 Keizer, 1999, 2.
613 Homer, Iliad, 24.725.
614 Plato, *Timaeus*, 37 D; in Homeric poems Aion relates to the human soul (Stamatellos, 2007,95).
615 Alföldi, 1997, 135.
616 Bowerstock, 1990, 25; Nonnus, *Dionysiaca*, XL.392-410.
617 Fossum, 1999, 308.
618 Turcan,1996, 12.
619 Ogawa, 1976, 658-682; Levi, 1944, 290; Beck, 2006, 153-189; Barton, 1994, 197-202; see sculpture from Housesteads depicting Mithras and zodiacal ring (CIMRM 860); Clauss 2000, 70-71.
620 Levi, 1944, 280.
621 Plotinus, The Enneads, III, 3.3 and 7,4; see also Porphyry's Cave of the Nymphs: Lamberton, 1983.
622 Clauss, 2000, 165; the mosaic from the Mithraeum of Felicissimus at Ostia includes the sickle of Saturn (CIMRM, I, 299,11).
623 Miguélez- Cavero, 2013, 353.

aged figure and there is a reference to Aion as "Circling time rolling the wheel of the four-season year".[624] For Nonnus, the Seasons are inextricably linked with Aion and have a clear cosmic function as they serve as guardians to the gates of heaven, which is how they are presented in the Iliad.[625] In Books XI and XII, the Seasons are described in anthropomorphic form with symbols to represent their particular time of year.[626] In the Roman imperial period, the four seasons came to represent the four ages of cosmic time: iron, bronze, silver and gold.[627]

Aion and the Four Seasons on Roman Imperial Coinage before the third century AD

All coinage with representations of Aion or the four seasons is incredibly rare. An *aureus* of Hadrian, struck at Rome, probably in AD 121, depicts the figure of Aion within a zodiacal circle, holding a globe on which is a phoenix (Figure 117). Strack recorded around one hundred known examples[628] and this example, which recently appeared at auction, clearly shows the zodiacal detail on the ring in which Aion stands. The reverse inscription SAEC AVR links it firmly to the claim of new Golden Age.[629] The symbolism of the Phoenix, linked to cyclical time, is discussed in Chapter 5.3. The coin may have been issued in relation to the founding of the *Natalis Urbis Romae Aeternae* and the commencement of the building of the *Templum Urbis* in AD 121 as discussed in Chapter 2.1.[630] The image of Aion within a zodiacal wheel represents the renewal of the Golden Age which is of limitless extension. [631]

Figure 117: Aureus of Hadrian (RIC II Part 3,2019 No 2840) © NAC Auction 92 part 1, May 2016

624 Nonnus, *Dionysiaca*, XXXVI, 422.

625 Miguélez- Cavero, 2013, 356; Homer, *Iliad*, 8.393.

626 Nonnus, *Dionysiaca*, XI, 485-521; e.g. summer carries a sickle (line 502). For the development of the personification of the Seasons see Bremmer, 2013, 161-178. The four seasons frequently appear on Roman mosaics.

627 Pollini, 1992, 296; Manilius, *Astronomica*, 2.398-405; Ovid, *Metamorphoses*, I, 89 – 150 (see Appendix III); Censorinus, *De Die Natali*, XVIII, 35ff.

628 Strack, 1933, 78.

629 Abdy, 2019, 37.

630 Hekster and Zair, 2008, 109.

631 Cohen, 2014, 17.

A similar figure of Aion in a zodiacal circle is depicted on a silver plate known as the Parabiagio Patera (probably 4th Century AD).[632] Rather than the phoenix on a globe, Aion holds a sceptre (Figure 118). The design also includes the four seasons and the figure of Tellus.

Figure 118: Aion on the Parabiagio Patera (4th century AD?) Civico Museo Archaeologico di Milano; Wikipedia image © Giovanni Dall'Orto

Aion, in this image, is shown holding a long sceptre, in a zodiacal circle being upheld by Atlas. Here, Aion appears with the figure of Attis whose death and resurrection are central to another myth about cyclical renewal. Once again, Aion and the seasons represent symbols of cosmic cycles and temporal renewal.[633]

It is thought that Antoninus Pius may have celebrated the Saecular Games on the occasion of Rome's 800th anniversary in AD 148.[634] He issued medallions whose subjects include the foundation myths of Rome along with representations of the four seasons (Figure 105).[635]

Marcus Aurelius issued a medallion in around AD 166 from Rome, which depicted his sons Commodus and Annius Verus on the obverse and reverse inscription of TEMPORVM FELICITAS (happiness of the times) with the four seasons depicted as children, each holding attributes of their particular time of year (Figure 119). While, at one level, the image could be seen as simply representing a single year, the image can also be seen as a dynastic statement of the blessings brought about by a new age in the context of cyclical time.

632   See LIMC 1.1, 399-411 for images of Aion.
633   Cohen, 2014, 18.
634   Levick, 2014,102.
635   Gnecchi 1912, II, 31 and 97; see also Gnecchi III, 137.

Figure 119: Medallion of Marcus Aurelius (Gnecchi, 1912, II, p44/1) © British Museum: 1872,0709.403

The four seasons are represented on a circular altar found on the site of the Gardens of Sallust in Rome (Figure 120). They are portrayed as winged male cherubs each carrying seasonal attributes.[636] On the left, Summer holds a sickle and Spring holds a basket of fruit and a garland.[637]

Figure 120: Details from the Four Seasons Altar, © Martin von Wagner Museum, Würzburg

636 For other Roman representations of the four seasons see Boschung, 2013, 179-200. See also LIMC V.1,1981,503-538.

637 See Galinksy, 1982, 459-460 on the development of images of the 'Horae'.

Commodus declared that in his reign a Golden Age had dawned[638] and minted coins and medallions accordingly.

Figure 121: Medallion of Commodus (Gnecchi,1912, II, no.75 p60/75) © *British Museum: 1873,0303.11*

The reverse of a bronze medallion (Figure 121), minted in Rome, depicts Aion standing in the centre with a sceptre in his left hand. His right hand rests on a zodiacal circle through which run personifications of the four seasons. On the left side stands a small figure with a cornucopia who represents a *genius* of plenty. The iconography can be interpreted as the bounty of a new Golden Age brought about by cyclical time.[639]

Commodus also minted a medallion depicting Tellus and the four seasons (Figure 113).[640] Given that Commodus also issued coins showing only the four seasons[641], this may be an example of coinage depicting a smaller aspect of complex iconography which could only be portrayed in full on a large medallion.[642]

The image of Aion and the four seasons survive on many surviving Roman mosaics.[643] Figure 122 shows the third century AD mosaic from Sentinum in Italy[644] with Aion as a young man standing inside a zodiacal circle. The four seasons as cherubs cluster around the reclining figure of Tellus (see chapter 5.4). The mosaic was found in a building containing a Mithraeum and the possible connections between Mithras and cyclical time have been mentioned above.[645]

---

638 Cassius Dio, 73.15.

639 Asolati, 2015,192.

640 Gnecchi 1912, II, 131.

641 RIC III, 382.

642 Bastien and Metzger, 1977, 214.

643 Levi, 1944, 269-274; Asolati, 2015, 189-202.

644 Watson, 2012, 198.

645 Chapter 5.2 and the Introduction.

Figure 122: Sentinum mosaic (3rd century AD) Glyptothek Museum Munich; image by permission from Wikimedia BibiSan Pol 2007.

The iconography of Aion and the Four Seasons on Roman Imperial Coinage in the third century AD

The coinage of Julia Domna which features Tellus and the four seasons is discussed in chapter 5.1 above. Septimius Severus issued coins from Rome, just after the celebration of the Saecular Games in AD 204, in the name of both of his sons, with a reverse inscription FELICIA TEMPORA (fortunate times) and a depiction of the four seasons (Figures 123, 124).[646] The attributes of each can clearly be seen and are described at Figure 126.

Figure 123: Denarius of Geta (RIC IV, 41) © British Museum :1946,1004.873

---

646 RIC IV 41: coin of Geta.

Figure 124: Denarius of Caracalla (RIC IV, 153) © Hunterian Museum:GLAHM 28572

The last of the Severan dynasty was the youthful Alexander Severus (AD 222-235). He issued a medallion in Rome (Figure 125) which is similar to that of Commodus (Figure 121). The obverse shows the emperor and his mother Julia Mammea. On the reverse, an older, seated Aion is depicted holding a short sceptre and who turns the wheel of time, through which the seasons pass, to bring back the Golden Age. Aion could be represented as an old or young man.[647]   He is being crowned by a winged figure of Victory There is another figure standing on his other side holding a long sceptre, usually identified as Felicitas. The inclusion of victory in the image may reflect the need to demonstrate success in battle at a time when the Empire was threatened in both the east and west.[648]

Figure 125: Medallion of Alexander Severus (Gnecchi 1912, II p85/12) © British Museum: 1877,0503.3

There is then a gap in the third century before Aion or the four seasons are seen again on known coinage. The interest that Philip I showed in the zodiacal circle is discussed in chapter 2.2 and mention should be made of the reference

647 Bijovsky, 2007, 149; Davies, 2004,97.
648 Southern, 2001, 81.

in the Thirteenth Sybilline Oracle [649] and the mosaic depicting Aion and the zodiacal circle at Philippopolis, illustrated at Figure 49.

Trebonianus Gallus (AD 251-253) issued a bronze medallion depicting the four seasons and a reverse inscription of SAECVLI FELICITAS (Figure 126). The attributes of each season can be clearly seen here: spring carries a basket of flowers, summer holds a sickle, autumn holds a hare and a *patera* of fruit, winter carries a hare and a *pedum* (crook) with two birds.

Figure 126: Medallion of Trebonianus Gallus - image from Gnecchi, 1912, II, p 102/5

The inscription on this medallion links to the good fortune that a returning Golden Age brings. For other Golden Age iconography on the coinage of Trebonianus Gallus see Figures 51 and 142.

Tacitus (AD 275-275) issued a bronze medallion showing the seated emperor with his hand on the zodiacal circle (Figure 127). This is similar to the design of Alexander Severus (Figure 125) but this time with the reverse inscription AETERNITAS AVG. Rather than the general message of 'fortunate times', the more specific inscription relates the image more strongly to the eternity of cyclical time and a return to the Golden Age. See Figure 94 for a coin of Tacitus with the inscription FELICITAS SAECVLI.

Figure 127: Medallion of Tacitus image from Gnecchi, 1912, III p66/12

649 Potter, 1990, 171, (lines 64-7).

Probus (AD 276-283) also employed the iconography of Aion and the four seasons. He issued a quinarius from Ticinum which has the reverse inscription [FE]LICIA TEMPORA and the four seasons (Figure 128). The design is remarkably similar to the Severan *denarii* above.

Figure 128: Quinarius of Probus (RIC 262 var.) © NAC Auction 78, Lot 1110, May 2014

Probus also issued a gold medallion from Siscia (Figure 129) which reverts to the design of the Commodus medallion (Figure 121). The reverse inscription is TEMP FELICITAS and shows the design of Aion with sceptre in left hand and his right hand holding the zodiacal wheel through which process the four seasons. Facing them is a small male figure holding a cornucopia. The iconography can, once again, be seen to represent the claim of a bountiful new Golden Age brought about through cyclical time.[650]

Figure 129: Medallion of Probus (Gnecchi 1912, I p10/6) © Bibliothèque Royale de Belgique

Another medallion (Figure 130) of Probus shows the four seasons on the reverse with the legend SAECVLI FELICITAS. Again, the Golden Age message through the felicity of the new age is portrayed.

---

650 Toynbee, 1934, 142, note 3; Davies, 2004, 97.

It is thought these medallions may have been produced as donatives for the triumphs in Rome in AD 281/282; this may have been an appropriate occasion to claim the peace of a Golden Age, having waged war to bring it about.[651]

Figure 130: Medallion of Probus - image from Gnecchi, 1912 II, p119/37

Carus and Carinus (AD 283-285) issued a medallion with the four seasons and a reverse inscription SAECVLI FELICITAS. The only known example is in a poor state of preservation (Figure 131).

Figure 131: Medallion of Carus and Carinus (Gnecchi 1912, II, p.121/1) Paris BNF 574 © Sylviane Estiot, CNRS.

Diocletian (AD 285-305) also employed the iconography of the four seasons on a quinarius, as Probus had done, from a mint at Ticinum (Figure 132).[652] The difference here is that the obverse shows Diocletian with the bust of Sol, which is highly appropriate for the cosmic image on the reverse, as Sol was thought to drive the seasons.[653]

---

651 Hedlund, 2008, 83. For the claim to bring Golden Age peace through war see: Augustus, *Res Gestae*, 13: *parta victoriis pax* (peace through victory); see also Galinsky, 1996,107.

652 It has been argued that the mint at Ticinum was probably set up to provide donative coins for distribution by the emperor in Rome: Estiot, 2004, 79.

653 For Sol's association with the Augustan Golden Age myth see discussion at Figure 108, Chapter 5.1.

Figure 132: Quinarius of Diocletian (RIC V 239) © British Museum ref.: 1947,0622.1

Figure 133 shows an image of Sol, with his whip, from the pediment of the Temple of Jupiter at Diocletian's Palace in Split. See Figure 67 for an image of Diocletian with Aion.

Figure 133: Figure of Sol from the Temple of Jupiter at Diocletian's Palace, Split (3rd/4th century AD) © G Barker

The usurper emperor Carausius (AD 286-293) also used this iconography (Figure 134). Given the apparently extensive use of Golden Age iconography on his coinage (see chapter 6) it is likely that this design was part of the promised return of a Golden Age through cyclical time.

Figure 134: Radiate of Carausius (RIC V 1016) © Private collection

Fourth century postscript

As an image of cyclical time returning the Golden Age, the zodiacal wheel continued in numismatic iconography into the fourth century as illustrated by this *aureus* of Constantine which is dated AD 316 from the mint at Ticinum (Figure 135). The reverse has the inscription is RECTOR TOTIVS ORBIVS and shows the emperor being crowned by victory standing right. As the emperor's hand rests on a zodiacal ring, the image portrays Constantine (AD 306 – 337) not only as the 'restorer of the whole world' but also as the restorer of the Golden Age.[654]

Figure 135: Aureus of Constantine (RIC VII 54) © British Museum: 1861,1113.2

The four seasons also continued in use as part of the iconography of a returning Golden Age in the fourth century AD as on this solidus of Constantine, also from Ticinum in the year AD 316 (Figure 136). This coin shows remarkable consistency of design of the four seasons and their attributes with the third century representations.[655]

Figure 136: Solidus of Constantine (RIC VII p. 366) © Ashmolean Museum, Oxford: ref. HCR4854

654 Asolati, 2015, 189-200.
655 See also a gold Medallion of Licinius with the same reverse RIC VII 31 British Museum: 1964,1204.1.

Summary

The appearance of Aion in the Roman imperial era seems to reflect a renewed preoccupation with concepts of time and cyclical time in particular.[656] The Augustan Saecular Games were fundamentally based on the idea of a cyclical Golden Age returning through renewal of cosmic time. The third century saw an explosion of interest in these concepts of cyclical time, partly fuelled by the Neoplatonic and Gnostic writers and so-called mystery religions. There are many images of Aion and the seasons in Roman art which tend to support this interest.

The coinage from the third century which depicts Aion and the four seasons is very rare indeed. This perhaps serves to support the argument, made in the introduction, that the concepts of a Golden Age were perhaps aimed only at an "inner circle" of the imperial court. Where the four seasons and Aion appear on coinage, they can be seen to represent at one level 'the return of fortunate times', but they can also be seen to be part of the iconography of a promised Golden Age returning through cyclical time.

5.3 The iconography of the Phoenix

Background to the Phoenix as a symbol of the Golden Age and Aeternitas

The history of the myth of the phoenix is complex and, like the Golden Age myth itself, stems from different sources over different times.[657] At the beginning of the reign of Seleucus I, in 312 BC, it appears that the phoenix had come to symbolise the return of a Golden Age when a new ruler took charge at the start of the Great Year.[658] Plato was among the first to define the Great Year in the Timaeus[659] and Cicero restated this concept of Plato.[660] Cicero noted that the calculation of the period of the Great Year was hotly disputed. So computations, at different times during the classical period, range from 1 to 7,006 years and even 972 human generations.[661]

Herodotus had linked the appearance of the Phoenix in Egypt to a 500 year cycle[662] while Tacitus, who also placed it appearance in Egypt, said that the phoenix appeared every 1,461 years.[663] The latter period became identified with "Sothic Period", an astronomical interval based on the heliacal rising of Sirius

---

656 Cohen, 2014,15.

657 Van den Broek, 1972.

658 Van den Broek, 1972,104; Manilius cited by Pliny, *Historia Naturalis*, X.2.

659 Plato, *Timaeus* 39.

660 See Introduction and Chapter 1.

661 Van den Broek, 1972, 72.

662 Herodotus, Histories, II, 73.

663 Tacitus, *Annales*, VI, 28; Tacitus was a member of the *quindecemviri* at the time of the Saecular Games of Claudius on the 800th anniversary of the founding of the City (Tacitus, *Annales*, XI.11).

coinciding with the Nile flood.[664] Censorinus, whose work "*De Die Natali*" has been discussed in the introduction, also highlighted the confusion surrounding the calculation of the Great Year.

Pliny the Elder said the phoenix came from Ethiopia, India and Arabia and lived 540 years. He cites Manilius in equating the bird's appearance with the cyclical concept of the Great Year.[665] Pliny records the appearance of a dubious phoenix in the Roman forum when Claudius celebrated the Saecular Games.[666] Aurelius Victor was later to record it as a fact that the phoenix had appeared in Egypt during the reign of the emperor Claudius (AD 41-54).[667]

The symbolism of the phoenix as the start of a new era brought in by the emperor was used by Martial after a fire in AD 80, in an epigram dedicated to Domitian:

"As the flames renew the nest of the Assyrian phoenix, whenever the solitary bird has lived through its ten centuries so Rome, renewed, has put off her former old age, and has herself assumed the looks of her guardian." [668]

The word *saecula*, here translated as centuries, is significant as Domitian was to celebrate the Saecular Games in AD 88 which ritualised the dawn of a new Golden Age under his rule.

In AD 118, Hadrian struck gold coinage to commemorate the deified Trajan with the inscription DIVVS TRAIANVS PATER on the obverse and a radiate phoenix on the reverse.[669] As well as marking the eternity of the divine Trajan, Hadrian was also advertising the fact that his reign marked the start of a new age.[670]

Chapter 5.1 discusses the *aureus* (Figure 117) which Hadrian struck in AD 121/122 showing Aion in a zodiacal circle, holding a globe surmounted by a phoenix with the exergue legend SAEC AVR, standing for *saeculum aureum*.[671] This image links the phoenix to the renewal of cyclical time in the context of a new Golden Age.[672] During Hadrian's reign the concept of *Aeternitas* also came to be linked with the Golden Age, as discussed above.[673]

---

664 Evans, 2008, 192.

665 Pliny, *Natural History*, X.2.

666 Pliny, *Natural History*, X.3.

667 Aurelius Victor, *De Caesaribus*, 4.14.

668 *"Qualiter Assyrios renovant incendia nidos, una decem quotiens saecula vixit avis, taliter exuta est veterem nova Roma senectam et sumpsit vultus preasidis ipsa sui."* Martial, Epigrams, 5.7.1-2. (translation in Bohn).

669 RIC II 343, 27/28.

670 Abdy, 2019, 37.

671 RIC II, 356 no. 136.

672 Hollard and Lòpez, 2014, 17-18.

673 Anderson, 1986, 121.

The ability of the phoenix to regenerate meant that it also represented immortality for members of the imperial family. On coinage, the phoenix was specifically identified with *Aeternitas*. In AD 141, Antoninus Pius was to strike several coin denominations in memory of the deified Faustina. These bore the legend DIVA FAVSTINA on the obverse and a reverse inscription of AETERNITAS with a female figure of *Aeternitas* holding a phoenix on a globe with a nimbus.[674] Faustina's death is said to have coincided with the start of a new Sothic period and was therefore linked with this renewal of cosmic time.[675] Similar coinage was issued by Marcus Aurelius in AD 176-180 in memory of the later deified Faustina I. There were two types of reverse inscription: AETERNITAS and also MATER CASTRORVM.[676] In this context, the phoenix represents the eternity accorded to the deified Empress but can also be linked to the eternity of the dynasty of which she was part.[677]

The third century written sources

Despite the paucity of surviving contemporary written sources, it is not difficult to find references to the phoenix in third century literature that survives. It was such a powerful symbol of cyclical time that it seems to have been recognised universally by different sections of society. As well as a symbol used by the Roman Imperial government, it was cited by Neoplatonists, Jews and Christians, among others.

The extraordinary book, '*The Life of Apollonius of Tyana*', was apparently commissioned from Philostratus by Julia Domna.[678] Among the many exotic creatures that appear in this fabulous tale, the phoenix is described as:

> "*The bird which visits Egypt every five hundred years, but the rest of that time it flies about in India; and it is unique in that it gives out rays of sunlight and shines with gold;*" [679]

From the writings of Eusebius, there is a reference that Porphyry had commented that Herodotus's version of the phoenix myth was taken from the Hecataeus of Miletus. [680]

The early Christian community had already adopted the phoenix as a symbol of the rebirth of the soul. So Tertullian was already using a well-known symbol when he referred to the phoenix as a symbol for resurrection.[681]

---

674 E.g. RIC III no. 1105, 161, 162.

675 Evans R, op. cit., 193.

676 RIC III: 740, 751.

677 Charlesworth, 1936, 124.

678 Anderson, 1986, 121.

679 Philostratus, Life of Apollonius of Tyana, Book III Chapter 49 (translation by F Conybeare)

680 Eusebius, *Praeparatio Evangelica*, X, 3.16.

681 Tertullian, *De Resurrectione Mortuorum*, 13.4.

Third Century AD Roman Imperial coinage

The first time the phoenix appears on Severan coinage is on the reverse of *denarius* issued in Julia Domna's name (Figure 137). The reverse shows the empress, seated, holding a phoenix on a globe with two military standards in front of her. It was probably issued from Rome in the late second century or early third century AD.

Figure 137: Denarius of Julia Domna (RIC IV 1, 568) © British Museum: 1928,1101.22

Figure 138: Aureus of Faustina I (RIC III 751) © British Museum: 1867,0101.730

The coin was issued in line with attempts to link her to both the older and younger Faustinas (Figure 138). Julia Domna was awarded the title Mater Castrorum in AD 195 following a precedent set by Faustina I.[682] The granting of this title coincided with Septimius Severus's adoption into the Antonine family, as the son of Marcus Aurelius.[683] This appears to have been a further attempt to reinforce his claim to the purple by providing links to a previous Imperial dynasty. As well as linking Julia Domna to Faustina, the phoenix in this context may also be an attempt to symbolise the divinity of the living empress.

Following Julia Domna's imitative use of the phoenix, it appears on a bronze medallion of the next empress whose family celebrated the Saecular Games. Just one example of Otacilia Severa is recorded by Gnecchi, where the reverse inscription is TEMPORVM FELICITAS (Figure 139). The reverse image shows Otacilia with two children, Felicitas holding a *caduceus* on one

682 Lusnia, 1995, 122.
683 Cassius Dio, *Historia Romana* LXXVI.7.

side and Aeternitas standing on her other side holding a transverse sceptre and a phoenix on a globe. The phoenix here provides a further indication that the Millennial Saecular Games of AD 248 were intended to bring about 'fortunate times' through the cyclical return of the Golden Age which the phoenix represents.

Figure 139: Medallion of Otacilia Severa - image from Gnecchi, 1912, II p 96/ 4

The next recorded appearance of the phoenix on coinage is for Trebonianus Gallus (AD 251 -253).

Figure 140: Sestertius of Trebonianus Gallus (RIC IV 102) © *British Museum: R4022*

Coinage bearing the reverse inscription AETERNITAS AVGG and a female personification of Aeternitas holding a phoenix on a globe (Figures 140, 142) was issued from Rome in different denomonations. [684]

Volusian, Trebonianus Gallus's son and co-ruler, also issued gold coinage with the phoenix and globe symbol and the legend *AETERNITAS* (Figure 141). It is interesting to note that the Rome mint issued coins of the same type with the inscription *AETERNITAS,* and the phoenix and globe reverse, while the Antioch mint issued coins with the legend *SAECVLVM NOVVM.*[685]

---

684 *Aureus*: RIC IV, 17; radiate (antoninianus): RIC IV, 30; *Sestertius*: RIC IV, 102.
685 Figure 50.

Figure 141: Aureus of Volusian (RIC IV, 154) © British Museum: 1867.0101.806

There may be a precedent for the iconography of the phoenix on coins of Trebonianus Gallus and his son Volusian. It has been asserted that the Jewish revolt in Hadrian's reign appeared to shake the peace of whole empire and the claim to have restored peace was underlined by return of a Golden Age.[686] This was one possible reason why Hadrian issued the *aureus* with the figure of Aion holding a phoenix on a globe (Figure 117). Augustus had first used Golden Age messages to reassert peace after a period of discord, and it may have been a pattern repeated by others.

Given the circumstances of the accession of Trebonianus Gallus, there would have been a similar need for reassurance of continuity and peace following the shock of Decius and his son both being killed in battle, the first Roman emperors to die in this context.[687] With father and son both using the same coin design, it is also clear that a dynastic message was intended to be read in conjunction with the implied symbolism of eternal renewal through cyclical time. [688] The fact that both father and son also issued coinage declaring a *saeculum novum* would indicate that the peace of a Golden Age renewal was symbolised by the phoenix on a globe.

Figure 142: Radiate of Trebonianus Gallus (RIC IV 30) © Private collection

In the Cunetio hoard the *Aeternitas* types, with phoenix and globe, of Trebonianus Gallus and Volusian account for approximately 3% of the coins of

---

686 Quet, 2004, 119.
687 Aurelius Victor, De *Caesaribus*, 29.
688 Dowling, 2004, 179.

Trebonianus Gallus and Volusian combined. The Dorchester hoard contains a smaller proportion of the same type of coin for Trebonianus Gallus (2.3%) with no such coins of Volusian. [689]

Following on from Trebonianus Gallus and Volusian, the same reverse coin design was used in the short-lived reign of Aemilianus (AD 253) and appears on his radiates and *sestertii* (Figures 143 and 144).

Figure 143: Sestertius of Aemilianus (RIC IV, 55)   © British Museum: R4090

Aemilianus also struck coins with a figure of *Roma* holding a phoenix on a globe but with the reverse inscription ROMAE AETERNAE. As discussed above, this reverse inscription is commonly found on coins of the third century and refers to *Roma Aeterna* as a personification of divine status; but nowhere else is it found on coinage with the phoenix and the globe. Philip I featured *Roma Aeterna* as the main deity in his Saecular Games (Chapter 2.2). The cult became inextricably linked with the emperor, and so adding the symbolism of the phoenix on the globe links the promise of eternal renewal through loyalty to both the empire and emperor.[690]

Figure 144: Radiate of Aemilianus (RIC IV, 9)   © CNG Auction 75, Lot 1111, May 2007

689 Besley and Bland, 1983.
690 Hedlund, 2008, 145; see also MacMullen, 1966, 157.

It is a matter of supreme irony, therefore, that the reign of Aemilianus lasted little more than three months and may explain why the phoenix was not used on coins for several years to come.

During the 'Gallic Empire', Tetricus I issued *aurei* from Trier in AD 273 with the reverse inscription AETERNITAS AVGG and the figure of Aeternitas holding a phoenix in one hand and raising her skirt with the other (RIC 206).[691] Only three examples of this coin are known. [692]

The phoenix reappears on imperial coinage ten years later (Figure 145) on the coins of Carinus (AD 283-285) once again with the legend AETERNITAS.

Figure 145: Radiate of Carinus (RIC IV 244) © CNG e-auction 245, Lot 368, December 2010

The image, on late third century coinage, of the phoenix on a globe, combined with the inscription *Aeternitas*, can be seen as a message of continuity of empire through the ruling dynasty. Trebonianus Gallus and Volusian also issued coins with the inscription *SAECVLVM NOVVM*, linking the *Aeternitas* message to a Golden Age renewal. In the short and chaotic rule of the Caran dynasty, with Carus alleged to have been killed by lightning,[693] perhaps there was again an urgent need for a symbol of continuity and renewal.

It should be noted that on all the later third century coinage, the reverse inscription that accompanies the image is AETERNITAS AVGG, i.e. "the eternity of the Augusti". Once again, this was probably intended to underscore a dynastic message of continuity.

---

691 RIC 206; Mairat 759/1.

692 Mairat, 2014, 741.

693 Eutropius, *Breviarum*, Book IX, 18.

Figure 146: Radiate of Diocletian (RIC V 204) © Gitbud and Nauman Auction 23, Lot 956, October 2014

The last appearance of the phoenix on third century coinage is on a rare issue of Diocletian from the mint at Ticinum (Figure 146). Once again, the reverse inscription is AETERNITAS. Maximian issued a similar coinage from the same mint.[694] It can be argued that the phoenix on a globe appeared on coins in the late third century in times of crisis and uncertainty when a powerful symbol, readily recognised, could seek to provide reassurance about continuity and the promise of everlastingly renewed peace and prosperity.

The Phoenix represented in Roman Art

Many of the representations of the phoenix in classical and early Christian art have been catalogued by Van den Broek. [695] The mosaics at Piazza Armerina, which are generally dated around the late third or early fourth century AD, provide more than one example of the phoenix. Figure 147 shows a Phoenix in flames on a corridor mosaic in an apse depicting Ethiopia, one of the legendary homes of the phoenix.

Figure 147: Phoenix in flames from a corridor mosaic, Piazza Armerina, photo by G Barker

---

694 RIC, V, 542.

695 Van den Broek, 1972, 425 – 464.

Figure 148 shows the radiate phoenix from an Orpheus mosaic at Piazza Armerina. Given the close connection of the phoenix with the Golden Age myth,[696] this image is in a particularly interesting context. At the head of the room with this mosaic is a statue of Apollo, the presiding god of the Augustan Golden Age. [697] The combination of Orpheus, who is twice mentioned in a prophetic context in Virgil's Fourth *Eclogue*, [698] with the statue of Apollo readily brings to mind the line from the Fourth *Eclogue*: "Your Apollo is now king!". [699]

Figure 148: Phoenix image from an Orpheus mosaic, Piazza Armerina photo by G Barker

Fourth Century postscript

The flowering of the phoenix as an emblem of the Golden Age was to come in the mid fourth century AD in a Christian context. As part of the celebration of the eleven hundredth anniversary of Rome, in AD 348, coinage was struck by the emperor Constans (AD 337-350) which incorporated the phoenix on a globe, the Christian CHI RHO symbol on a standard (*labarum*) and the reverse inscription FEL TEMP REPARATIO or 'restoration of blessed times' (Figure 149). [700] As the eschatological concept of the ending of the Roman Empire after twelve *saecula* still endured, "it was necessary for the emperor not merely to inaugurate a new and happy *saeculum* but offer some assurance that it would in

---

696 Ware, 2012, 112.

697 Miller, 2009, 253.

698 Virgil, Fourth *Eclogue*, Lines 54 and 56.

699 *Tuum iam regnat Apollo:* Virgil, Fourth *Eclogue*, Line 10.

700 Note also radiate issues from the Trier mint with a phoenix reverse in AD 348 – 350: RIC VIII p154.

fact not be the last".[701] The phoenix on a globe therefore continued to represent an assurance of everlastingly renewed *saecula*. Furthermore, the court writer Claudian incorporated copious Golden Age references into his writings and the phoenix would come, once again, to symbolise Rome's new age of gold.[702]

Figure 149: Nummus of Constans (RIC VIII 77)   © British Museum: 2011,4021.3

701   Kent J, 1966, 85.
702   Christiansen P and Sebesta J, 1985, 208, 212.

6

A CASE STUDY OF A 'USURPER EMPEROR' : GOLDEN AGE ICONOGRAPHY ON THE COINAGE OF CARAUSIUS

The concept of 'usurpers' and imperial legitimation in the third century AD

In the later third century AD, the instability caused by enormous military pressures on the frontiers produced frequent rival claims for the imperial purple.[703] These imperial candidates are generally classified as usurpers but, as Alaric Watson has pointed out, "It is both meaningless and misleading to attempt to divide those who claimed imperial power in the third century into 'legitimate emperors' and mere 'usurpers' based solely on the accident of whether the would-be emperor ever received the recognition of the senate in Rome." [704] Some usurpers may simply have been seeking to defend a particular province even though the act of minting their own coin was seen as high treason.[705] The senate's approval became less important as the century progressed [706] and key military support became one of the essential pillars for imperial authority to rule.[707]

From the end of the second century AD many of the "legitimate" emperors started as usurpers who entered a contest for power. [708] In this context, it has been shown that "coinage was an ideal vehicle for communication aimed at specific audiences, such as the military..., through which an emperor could symbolically represent himself and his leadership." [709]

The political instability of the third century AD meant that anyone who proclaimed himself emperor might employ a variety of approaches for legitimation. It has been observed that, "the self-legitimation of rebels is similar in kind to the self-legitimation of rulers and is cultivated for the

---

703 Southern, 2001, 412-413.

704 Watson, 1999, 5.

705 Potter, 2004, 250.

706 De Blois, 1976, 59.

707 Hedlund, 2008, 96.

708 Claes, 2015,15.

709 Claes, 2015, 16.

same reasons."[710] The Golden Age claims, as set down by Augustus, may have provided a useful means of legitimation for more than one "usurper" emperor.[711] As the written and epigraphic records are sparse, numismatic evidence is virtually the only record of these claims. Added to which, even if the "usurper" was temporarily recognised as a legitimate co-ruler,[712] once these rival claimants were assassinated, a form of *damnatio memoriae* would ensure the removal of any records that might have existed.[713]

The Written Sources for Carausius

In terms of contemporary writings, references to Carausius can be found in the extravagant oratory of the panegyrics of late Roman emperors known as the *Panegyrici Latini*.[714] While his name is never mentioned in these highly embroidered court eulogies, he is generally referred to as "the enemy" or "the pirate".[715] His breakaway empire in Britain was clearly a major thorn in the side of Diocletian and Maximian.[716] Eutropius describes Carausius as hailing from *Menapia* (modern day Belgium) and as a man of great military experience.[717] Aurelius Victor and Eutropius both refer to Carausius's official commission from Maximian to put together a fleet to contain the problem of seaborne raiders who infested the north coast of Europe.[718] These passages also refer to the allegation that he kept the pirate booty which should have been handed over to the Treasury, which explains why the panegyrics refer to him as a pirate. A similar sort of accusation was thrown at Postumus when he broke away to form the "Gallic Empire" and can, perhaps, be seen as a *topos* of imperial propaganda for "usurper" emperors.[719] The sources indicate that Carausius usurped imperial power and ruled as emperor of Britain for around seven years from AD 286-293.[720]

The Golden Age iconography of the coinage of Carausius

The coinage of Carausius is prodigious and has been described as "characterised by unusual and original coin designs." [721] Guy de la Bédoyère identified an

710   Barker, 2001, 99.

711   Uranius Antoninus issued a coin with a dated *cippus* and the inscription SAECVLARES AVGG (RIC IV 7) see Claes, 2015 46; for Pacatian's coinage see Brent, 2010, 160.

712   An example is Albinus being made co-ruler by Septimius Severus: Herodian, II. 5.3.

713   Varner, 2004, 213.

714   Nixon and Rodgers, 1994.

715   E.g. Nixon and Rodgers, op cit,120.

716   Webb, 1907, 9.

717   Eutropius, *Breviarum*, Book IX,13-14.

718   Aurelius Victor, *De Caesaribus*, Ch 39; Eutropius, *Breviarum*, Book IX (13).

719   Grünewald, 1999, 80-86; the term bandit (*latrona*) was often used against political enemies.

720   Williams, 2004, 8.

721   Mairat, 2014,151.

inscription on a Carausius medallion (Figure 150)[722] as Virgilian and as specifically from the Fourth *Eclogue*, one of the key sources for the Augustan Golden Age myth.

Figure 150: Medallion of Carausius (Toynbee 1986 Pl.XXX no. 4) © British Museum:1967,0901.

I.N.P.C.D.A. exactly correlates to line seven in Virgil's Eclogue which runs *"Iam nova progenies caelo demittitur alto"* (now a new generation descends from heaven on high).[723] De la Bedoyére realised that the preceding three word phrase from the *Eclogue* could explain the three letters which appear in the exergue of the majority of Carausius's silver coinage. The three letters are RSR, which correlates to the previous phrase in line six of the *Eclogue*: *"Redeunt Saturnia Regna"* (the reign of Saturn returns).[724] Only those with a high degree of literacy could have understood the Golden Age reference and this corroborates the idea, put forward in the introduction, that the intended message was essentially for a highly educated circle of those round the emperor.[725]

Figure 151 illustrates a *denarius* with RSR in the exergue and also has the reverse inscription RENOV ROMAN which is short for *"renovat romana"* (*romanitas* renewed). The reverse also appeared on the gold coinage of Carausius.[726] This highly distinctive inscription, together with the design of the wolf and twins Romulus and Remus, emphasises the desire to reassert the old

---

722 Toynbee, 1986, Pl.XXX no. 4.

723 Translation by H Fairclough; see Appendix I.

724 De la Bédoyère, 1998, 79. The idea had originally been put forward that RSR might stand for *Rationalis Summae Rei*: Casey, 1994, 76.

725 Hekster, 2003, 31; Casey, 1994, 48.

726 RIC V 534.

Roman values and traditions.[727] *Renovatio* also carries the meaning of rebirth which is highly appropriate in a Golden Age context.

Figure 151: Denarius of Carausius (RIC V 571) © Private collection

The resonant iconography of the wolf and twins, and its powerful link to the foundation of Rome, has been discussed above.[728] The coinage of Carausius emphasises faith in Roman traditions and Roman identity, including the Augustan Golden Age myth.[729] This is the most common design on Carausian silver coinage and comprises 17.6 % of all known specimens.[730]

The RSR initials also appear on rare radiate coinage of Carausius, and the more limited range of designs on these coins include the wolf and twins (Figure 152). This might indicate that, though rare, the coinage was intended for a broader audience and the iconography could be understood at a more general level.

Figure 152: Radiate of Carausius (RIC V 615) © British Museum: 1987,0647.407

---

727 "Nostalgic *Romanitas*" may have been aimed at homesick army officers and officials see: Claes, 2015, 16.

728 Figure 36, Chapter 2.2.

729 Estiot, 2012, 557; the same point is made for Septimius Severus: Rantala, 2013, 37.

730 Moorhead, RIC Carausius, forthcoming.

Early on in his reign, Carausius issued coins with the reverse inscription ROMAE AETERNAE showing the seated goddess Roma presenting victory to the emperor (Figure 153). As discussed in Chapter 2.2, *Roma Aeterna* was the principal deity promoted on the *saecvlvm novvm* coinage of Philip I. [731]

Figure 153: Radiate of Carausius (RIC V 390) © British Museum: 2012,4231.5

A rare silver coin was later produced (Figure 154) with the reverse inscription ROMAE AETERNAE and the image of the goddess Roma in her temple. This mirrors the design used by Philip I at the time of his Saecular Games (Figure 40). Only two specimens are known. [732]

Figure 154: Denarius of Carausius (RIC V 578) © British Museum: 1844,0425.2315

Allectus, who followed Carausius as the second ruler of the break-away "British Empire" from AD 293-296, also issued coins with this reverse.[733]

Carausius is one of the few emperors to issue coinage with an image of Ops, the wife of Saturn, the bringer of the Golden Age (Figure 155).[734] Not

731 Fowden, G. (2005) 557; see Chapter 2.2.

732 Moorhead, RIC Carausius, forthcoming.

733 RIC 40 and 113. The '*Allectus arcae galliarum*' was the title of an official at the Imperial Cult in Lugdunum who were professional financial administrators who came from the merchant classes (Drinkwater, 1983, 113). It may be that Allectus was one of these officials who became finance minister for Carausius. The contemptuous reference in the panegyrics to Gaulish merchants (*mercatoribus Gallicanis*) as followers of Carausian usurpation, may be a reference to Allectus (Pan Lat viii, 12).

734 Antoninus Pius issued coins with this reverse e.g. RIC 3 612.

only is Ops a goddess of the earth and fertility but Varro equates her with Terra Mater who is one of the principal goddesses to whom sacrifice is made in the rituals of the Saecular Games. [735] The reverse inscription OPIS IVI has been interpreted as "Ops of the invincible emperor Augustus." [736] It seems more likely that the reverse inscription was a misinterpretation of a coin of Pertinax where the reverse is OPI DIVI. [737] The coins of Carausius with the OPIS reverse appear only to have been produced in the early part of his reign and were produced by the travelling or so-called Rouen mint. [738]

Figure 155: Aureus of Carausius © Ashmolean Museum : HCR 3598

A *denarius* of Carausius appears to emphasise the messianic or prophetic approach to his rule (Figure 156). The reverse inscription EXPECTATE VENIES (come thou long awaited one) shows the emperor being greeted by the figure of Britannia. This phrase is closely mirrored in a Virgilian reference from the *Aeneid*: "*Quibus Hector ab oris exspectate venis*" (from what shores, Hector, do you come, long awaited one?). [739]

Figure 156: Denarius of Carausius (RIC V 554) © Private collection

---

735 Varro, *De Lingua Latina*, 5.64: Ops is called mother which is to say *Terra Mater* (Mother Earth): *et ideo dicitur Ops Mater, quod Terra Mater.*

736 Shiel, 1973, 166-168; see Moorhead, 2014,223.

737 RIC 3 8a.

738 Moorhead, 2014,222.

739 Virgil, *Aeneid*, Book II, 283 (translation G. Barker).

Both the Virgilian reference and the messianic quality of the inscription are of a piece with the Golden Age theme of *"Redeunt Saturnia Regna"*. The emperor on the obverse holds a globe in his right hand, which was traditionally seen as a symbol of the cosmos and eternity,[740] though by the third century it was also seen as an emblem of imperial rank. The reverse inscription EXPECTATE VENIES comprises around 9% of known Carausian silver coinage.[741]

This interpretation of the RSR exergue inscription on Carausian coinage has been treated with scepticism by some,[742] while others have endorsed it as "without a shadow of doubt correct".[743] The use of the Golden Age myth, as reinvented by Augustus, would seem to be a perfect vehicle for a usurper emperor claiming legitimacy in the late third century.

Following the discovery of the Linchmere hoard in 1928 one coin in particular (Figure 157) led to the claim that Carausius celebrated the Saecular Games.[744]

Figure 157: Radiate of Carausius (RIC V 393)   © British Museum: 1925, 0316.361

This coin features the familiar Saecular Games design with the reverse inscription SAECVLARES AVG and a *cippus* with a consular date of COS IIII. There are now four other known Carausian examples of this type of coin, one of which is illustrated at Figure 158. This reverse clearly shows it was struck

---

740 Hijmans, 2009, 75; Davies, 2004,87.

741 Moorhead, RIC Carausius, forthcoming.

742 Williams, 2004, 81; Williams doubts the authenticity of the Carausian medallion (Figure 150) though recent tests by the British Museum show the metal to date from the Roman period; see Barker, 2015,165.

743 Birley, 2005, 376; see also Estiot, 2012, 557.

744 Webb P, RIC V 2, 477; Webb assumed Carausius held the Saecular Games in London. The issue of provincially held Saecular Games has been tentatively supported by study of the inscriptions at Qasr al Bint, Petra, of Aiacius Modestus, a quindecemvir, from the time of Septimius Severus – see Várhelyi, 2010, 210; though these inscriptions may have been a provincial record of the Saecular Games held in Rome - Rowan, 2012, 65-67. See also speculation about provincial Saecular Games in *Hispania* in Stanley, 1994,235.

at the "C" mint and the designs from this mint are more closely associated the emperor.[745]

Figure 158:Radiate of Carausius (RIC V 393) © Private collection

No other dated *cippus* issues of the third century have the date COS IIII inscribed on them. So this is no slavish copy of an earlier emperor but a deliberate and specific dating of a coin which appears to follow the Augustan precedent of a dated *cippus*. The Frome hoard, discovered in 2010,[746] contains over 850 coins of Carausius and includes Saecular Games coin types which are similar to designs used by Philip I (Figure 159). Of the coins with the reverse legend SAECVLARES AVG, there are ten examples known of the coin with the lion reverse design and only one with the stag design.[747]

Figure 159: Reverses of two radiates of Carausius, Frome Hoard (unlisted) © British Museum

Carausius operated two main mints in Britain, one in London and the other being the C mint. The location of the C mint, if there was one, has not been identified.[748] But it is clear that the C mint produced coins that had greater individuality of design and which were much more personal to the emperor. It is entirely appropriate, therefore, that the SAECVLARES AVG coinage was produced by the C mint.

---

745 Moorhead, RIC forthcoming.
746 Moorhead, Booth, Bland, 2010, 22-31.
747 Moorhead, RIC forthcoming.
748 Casey, 1994, 84.

Carausian coinage which makes novel reference to *saecula* bringing back the Golden Age are the silver coins which have the reverse inscription VIRTVS SAECC and the design of a radiate lion with a thunderbolt in its mouth (Figure 160). The coin may encapsulate the Augustan concept that the personal qualities of the emperor (*virtus* being the peculiarly male quality of military excellence) are themselves key to bringing back the Golden Age.[749] The importance of *virtus* to the Augustan Golden Age myth is shown in Virgil's Fourth *Eclogue*, where the Golden Age cannot begin until the messianic figure has learnt the nature of *virtus*.[750] The *Carmen Saeculare* also highlights the importance of *virtus*.[751]

Carausius was not alone in claiming his *virtus* would bring a return of the Golden Age. It has been noted that in the late third century, several emperors, such as Tacitus and Florian,[752] used images on coins which depicted the Golden Age which the emperor would bring about by the force of his *virtus* (manly courage).[753]

This reverse design of the radiate lion with thunderbolt first appeared on the dated coinage of Caracalla and links to Alexander the Great (e.g. RIC 4, 273a and 571). It can be also seen on the dated coins of later emperors such as Postumus (RIC V, 1), Aurelian (RIC V, 1, 159), Probus (RIC V, 2, 616) Diocletian (RIC V, 4) and Maximian (RIC V, 344). The double CC in SAECC probably represents a plurality of the noun – as for example the double GG in AVGG represents Augusti.[754] So this coin inscription may, uniquely, refer to the plurality of the *saeculum* and, thus, the cyclical nature of the Golden Age message.

Figure 160: Denarius of Carausius (RIC V 592 var.) © Private collection

749 Galinsky, 1996 pp 84, 256.

750 Ware, 2012, 198.

751 Horace, *Carmen Saeculare*, line 42. See appendix II.

752 See Figures 94 and 95 Chapter 4.

753 Hedlund, 2008, 82.

754 Carausius issued coins with the obverse inscription AVGGG (e.g. RIC 143) which famously include the triple- headed issue with the inscription CARAUSIVS ET SVI FRATRES (RIC 1). This may have been a legitimising claim to be a local imperial colleague of Diocletian and Maximian: Claes, 2015, 18.

The radiate lion with thunderbolt is not only a reference to Alexander the Great[755] but has another Augustan link, as Augustus was often compared with Alexander. [756] The reverse design of a radiate lion on the coinage of the usurper Uranius has been similarly linked to a claim to be a new Alexander. [757] These coins may also represent part of the 'Alexandermania' of the third century AD.[758] Only three examples of this particular Carausius coin are known.[759]

A unique coin (Figure 161) features an obverse inscription of VIRTVS CARAVSI and the reverse features a large ship and the inscription PACATRIX AV (peace maker of the Augustus). As far as is known, this is the only known use of the word *pacatrix* on Roman coinage. Given that Carausius had been officially tasked with clearing the seas of pirates before he broke ranks, [760] this unusual word may in itself be a reference to Augustus who declared in his *Res Gestae* that he "pacified and protected the seas from pirates". [761] It may be that the ship is an image of the flag ship of the Carausian fleet[762] and that the letters CANC are connected with the name of the ship.[763] The obverse and reverse combined, again reinforce the message that through the *virtus* of Carausius (and this would include his naval skill as attested by historians)[764] the peace of a Golden Age is returning.

Figure 161: Radiate of Carausius (unlisted) © Ashmolean Museum: HCR 3632

755 Woods, 2018, 189-194.

756 Reed, 1998, 399-418.

757 Baldus, 1971,129.

758 Dahman, 2008, 522.

759 Another five known coin types have the radiate lion and thunderbolt design; Moorhead, RIC Carausius, forthcoming.

760 Eutropius, *Breviarum*, Book 9. 21.

761 Augustus, *Res Gestae*, 25.1: "*mare pacavi a praedonibus.*" This is the sole use of the verb *pacare* in this work.

762 Sutherland, 1937, 309.

763 The letters may stand for CANCER (the crab): Woods, 2012,66; Moorhead, RIC forthcoming. The letters may simply be a mintmark.

764 Aurelius Victor, *De Caesaribus*, Ch 39.

Peace and prosperity were two of the core messages of the Augustan Golden Age.[765] It has been estimated that over 70% of all the coinage of Carausius has a reverse inscription of PAX AVG (Figure 162).[766] This is an extraordinarily high figure for a single reverse inscription of any emperor.

Figure 162: Aureus of Carausius (unlisted) © British Museum ref: 2009,4112.1

In terms of the prosperity and plenty promised by a Golden Age, Carausius issues a coin type with completely novel iconography. The reverse inscription VBERITAS is well known in the third century but only Carausius produces these with a design of a milkmaid milking a cow (Figure 163). This extraordinary image may be a reference to Virgil's Georgics: *ubera vaccae lactea demittunt* (the cows' drooping milk-laden udders)[767] which precedes a reference to the Golden Age. It also brings to mind the image of the cow from the Ara Pacis of Augustus (Figure 106). This original design appears on over 3% of the known silver Carausian coinage.[768]

Figure 163: Denarius of Carausius (unlisted) © Private collection

---

765 See Introduction.

766 Williams, 1994, 71.

767 Virgil, Georgics II, 524-525; the image may also be a reference to the phrase in Horace's *Carmen Saeculare fertilis, frugum pecorisque tellus* (the earth, fruitful in crops and cattle); line 29 see Appendix II.

768 Moorhead, RIC Carausius, forthcoming.

The combination of this design and inscription incorporates a pun on the word *uber,* Latin for udder.[769] Vespasian issued coinage with a reverse design of the goatherd milking a goat (RIC 977) but with a different reverse inscription. The earlier emperors who employed this reverse inscription[770] used a rather more prosaic design of a female figure of *Uberitas* holding a purse and cornucopia.[771]

Summary

Carausius issued a great variety of remarkable coinage which included a novel range of iconography and inscriptions. A key inspiration for the legitimation of his reign appears to have been the Augustan Golden Age myth. While Carausius drew upon standard designs for his coinage, such as the dated *cippus,* he and his engravers, particularly those at the "C" mint, produced a wide range of original iconography. While the SAECVLARES AVG coinage is rare and presumably intended for an elite circle, the fact that the vast majority of his silver coinage and some radiates bear the inscription RSR indicates that a broader circle of educated, moneyed people may have been the intended audience. The only contemporary epigraphic evidence that survives from the reign of Carausius is a single inscription on a milestone.[772] So it is the extraordinary Carausian coinage that remains as a testament to his rule of seven years, a reign inspired by the Augustan Golden Age myth as a claim to legitimation.

---

769 Casey, 1994, 48.

770 e.g. Trajan Decius, RIC IV 3, 129 and Trebonianus Gallus RIC IV, 3 169.

771 E.g. Gallienus *aureus* RIC 5, 71.

772 RIB 2291 found near Carlisle.

7

CONCLUSION

"After Virgil had sung of the hero 'who should found again the Golden Age in fields once ruled by Saturn' the vision of that age haunted the Roman Empire along the whole of its course." [773]

The coinage of the third century AD bears out Mattingly's opinion, quoted above, as the iconography of the Golden Age can be identified on coinage throughout this period. Certain aspects of the imagery remained constant such as the dated *cippus* to record the rituals of the Saecular Games which ushered in a new Golden Age. The dated *cippus* design directly follows a precedent set by Augustus.

Just as the Golden Age myth itself was adapted and developed over the years, [774] so different iconography was employed in association with different reigns. Septimius Severus included representations of his patron deities, Hercules and Liber Pater, on his Saecular Games coinage. For Philip I, *Roma Aeterna* is the god most closely associated with the new *saeculum* on coins. Both emperors depict images of the emperor and family sacrificing at the Saecular Games as acts of piety that ushered in a new Golden Age.

Septimius Severus followed a number of precedents set by by Augustus including the date of his Saecular Games which were celebrated exactly two *saecula*, as laid down in the *Carmen Saeculare*, after the Augustan Games. As well as following the Augustan coin design of the dated *cippus*, the Severan coinage included issues which were similar to the Saecular Games coins of Domitian which showed ritual sacrifices. This type of image also appears on the medallions of Philip I for the Millennial Saecular Games. Philip I struck higher numbers of Saecular Games coins than any other emperor, and the image *Roma Aeterna* became an integral part of the Golden Age imagery on coins for the rest of the third century AD. As with other designs, the iconography was capable of more general interpretation, but it was frequently issued in conjunction with other coins that were linked to a Golden Age image. The larger issues of lower value coins, struck by Philip for the Saecular Games, show a series of animals which presumably represent the circus games which followed the three days of rituals set by Augustus.

---

773 Mattingly, 1947, 18.
774 Forsyth, 2012, 73; Barker, 1996,436.

It can be shown that Gallienus sought to emulate Augustus and portrayed aspects of the longed-for Golden Age on his coinage. While the image of Amalthea and baby Jupiter can be directly related to the Golden Age, in general, Gallienus appears to have adopted a more original, and perhaps mystical, approach to Golden Age designs on his coins. Under the Tetrarchs, Golden Age references on coins are much rarer but the myth is widely used in the panegyrics and these may link to specific coin and medallion issues.

It is possible to chart the frequent claim of a returning Golden Age by third century emperors through the extensive use of the phrase SAECVLI FELICITAS (good fortune of the *saeculum*) on coins. The variety of iconography that appears with the inscription included various images of Felicitas or the emperor advancing with spear and globe or portraits of the dynasty, for the Severans, and Diana Lucifera for Valerian and Gallienus. For the second half of the third century AD it has been observed that the 'return of the Golden Age' became "a recurrent theme in the coinages of the soldier emperors".[775]

Tellus, who is closely associated with the Augustan Golden age myth, appears on Severan coinage and probably that of Otacilia Severa. Aion, the god associated with cyclical time, makes rare, sporadic appearances on the coinage of the third century. His image mostly appears on medallions, where he holds a zodiacal circle through which walk four boys, representing the four seasons. It is likely that where the four seasons appear on smaller sized coinage this is a "cut down" version of the same image, though perhaps only those in the "inner circle" would appreciate the Golden Age reference. Again, the images should be seen in the context of other Golden Age iconography used by particular emperors. While no coin iconography of Aion survives from the time of Philip I, a contemporary written source (the Thirteenth Sybilline Oracle) and a mosaic from Philippopolis provide possible links between the emperor and this deity who was associated with the return of the Golden Age through cyclical time. On fourth century coinage, the image the four seasons and the zodiacal wheel of Aion continued to represent the return of the Golden Age.

The phoenix makes a brief appearance on the coinage of Julia Domna at the start of the third century in imitation of Antonine coinage and a single medallion of Otacilia Severa includes a phoenix. Then Trebonianus Gallus, who claims a new Golden Age on his SAECVLVM NOVVM coinage, strikes coins with an image of the phoenix with the reverse inscription AETERNITAS. The phoenix embodies the concept of cyclical time, and from the time of Claudius the phoenix had been firmly associated with the renewal of a new Golden Age. The phoenix appears on the coinage of certain emperors up to the end of the third century and then continues in use into the fourth century, where its association with the Golden Age is made even more explicit.

While the iconography of the Golden Age myth may have altered over time, the main reasons for claiming the return of the Golden Age did not essentially change from the time of Augustus. It can be argued that the need for

775 Hedlund, 2008, 80.

legitimation became ever more pressing as the third century progressed. The nature of the different layers of "crisis", or at least political instability, have been touched on earlier. With his version of the Golden Age myth, Augustus provided a language, both written and visual, through which an emperor could affirm the legitimation of his reign.[776] The need for communicating shared values to reinforce legitimacy has been well recognised.[777] In a nutshell, "Maintaining the legitimacy of the Roman emperor can be understood as a continuous communication of the legitimacy of the ruler to groups of interest".[778] The iconography of the coinage was one way in which this communication could be made. The legitimising power of Golden Age iconography is perhaps most graphically illustrated in the late third century AD by the extraordinary coinage of the usurper emperor Carausius.

Identifying the members of the inner Court circles or "groups of interest" must remain speculative but it is likely they included those close to the emperor, a range of key officials and a court which, in the later third century AD, probably comprised essentially senior military personnel.[779] The rarity of the majority of the coinage with Golden Age messages has been commented upon throughout this book. Medallions, which figure strongly in this context, were produced only in small numbers and probably chiefly intended as personal gifts from the emperor. All this tends to reinforce the notion that any intended communication was probably for the narrow audience of the emperor's inner Court circle.

One particular aspect of the Golden Age iconography on third century AD coinage that stands out is the emphasis on dynastic continuity. The claim that the Golden Age would continue with a dynastic successor was another precedent set by Augustus.[780] Time and again, emperors would feature iconography on coinage issued in the name of their son and heir to highlight the crown prince as "the bringer of a new Golden Age".[781] The most distinctive images in this context are to be found on the coinage of Gallienus.

The final word on the importance of the Saecular Games rituals as guarantors of a Golden Age should rest with Zosimus, writing in the 5th century AD:

> *"Experience assures us, that while these ceremonies were duly performed, according to the direction of the oracles, the empire was secure, and likely to retain its sovereignty over almost all the known world; and on the other hand, when they were neglected, about the time when Diocletian laid down the imperial dignity, it fell to decay, and degenerated insensibly into barbarism."* [782]

---

776 Alföldi, 1934, 3-118; Hölscher, 2000, 147-149; Zanker, 1987, 90, 209, 252.

777 Ando, 2000,77.

778 Hedlund, 2008, 17; Claes, 2015, 285.

779 Hedlund, 2008, 19.

780 Versnel, 1993, 205.

781 Rantala, 2017, 100; Alföldi, 1929, 270.

782 Zosimus, Historia Nova, Book 2. 7 (translation in Green and Chaplin).

APPENDIX I

VIRGIL: *ECLOGUE* IV

Sicelides Musae, paulo maiora canamus.
non omnis arbusta iuvant humilesque myricae;
si canimus silvas, silvae sint consule dignae.
Ultima Cumaei venit iam carminis aetas;

magnus ab integro saeclorum nascitur ordo. [5]
iam redit et Virgo, redeunt Saturnia regna,
iam nova progenies caelo demittitur alto.
tu modo nascenti puero, quo ferrea primum
desinet ac toto surget gens aurea mundo,
casta fave Lucina; tuus iam regnat Apollo.

Teque adeo decus hoc aevi, te consule, inibit, [11]
Pollio, et incipient magni procedere menses;
te duce, si qua manent sceleris vestigia nostri,
inrita perpetua solvent formidine terras.
ille deum vitam accipiet divisque videbit
 permixtos heroas et ipse videbitur illis
pacatumque reget patriis virtutibus orbem.

At tibi prima, puer, nullo munuscula cultu [18]
errantis hederas passim cum baccare tellus
mixtaque ridenti colocasia fundet acantho.
ipsae lacte domum referent distenta capellae
ubera nec magnos metuent armenta leones;
ipsa tibi blandos fundent cunabula flores.
occidet et serpens et fallax herba veneni
occidet; Assyrium vulgo nascetur amomum.

At simul heroum laudes et facta parentis [26]
iam legere et quae sit poteris cognoscere virtus,
molli paulatim flavescet campus arista
incultisque rubens pendebit sentibus uva
et durae quercus sudabunt roscida mella.

Pauca tamen suberunt priscae vestigia fraudis, [31]
quae temptare Thetin ratibus, quae cingere muris
oppida, quae iubeant telluri infindere sulcos.
alter erit tum Tiphys et altera quae vehat Argo

delectos heroas; erunt etiam altera bella
atque iterum ad Troiam magnus mittetur Achilles.

Hinc, ubi iam firmata virum te fecerit aetas,   [37]
cedet et ipse mari vector nec nautica pinus
mutabit merces; omnis feret omnia tellus.
non rastros patietur humus, non vinea falcem,
robustus quoque iam tauris iuga solvet arator;
nec varios discet mentiri lana colores,
ipse sed in pratis aries iam suave rubenti
murice, iam croceo mutabit vellera luto,
sponte sua sandyx pascentis vestiet agnos.

'Talia saecla' suis dixerunt 'currite' fusis   [46]
concordes stabili fatorum numine Parcae.

Adgredere o magnos—aderit iam tempus—honores, [48]
cara deum suboles, magnum Iovis incrementum.
aspice convexo nutantem pondere mundum,
terrasque tractusque maris caelumque profundum;
aspice, venturo laetantur ut omnia saeclo.

O mihi tum longae maneat pars ultima vitae,   [53]
spiritus et quantum sat erit tua dicere facta:
non me carminibus vincat nec Thracius Orpheus
nec Linus, huic mater quamvis atque huic pater adsit,
Orphei Calliopea, Lino formosus Apollo.
Pan etiam, Arcadia mecum si iudice certet,
Pan etiam Arcadia dicat se iudice victum.

Incipe, parve puer, risu cognoscere matrem;   [60]
matri longa decem tulerunt fastidia menses.
incipe, parve puer. qui non risere parenti,
nec deus hunc mensa dea nec dignata cubili est.

VIRGIL, VOL. I, translated by H. Rushton Fairclough, Loeb Classical
Library Volume 63, Cambridge Mass.: Harvard University Press, Copyright
© 1999 by the President amd Fellows of Harvard College. Loeb Classical
Library ® is a registered trademark of the President and Fellows of Harvard
College.

[1] Sicilian Muses, let us sing a somewhat loftier strain. Not everyone do
orchards and the lowly tamarisks delight. If your song is of the woodland, let
the woods be worthy of a consul.

[5] Now is come the last age of Cumaean song; the great line of the centuries begins anew. Now the Virgin returns, the reign of Saturn returns; now a new generation descends from heaven on high. Only do you, pure Lucina, smile on the birth of the child, under whom the iron brood shall at last cease and a golden race spring up throughout the world! Your own Apollo now is king!

[11] And in your consulship, Pollio, yes, yours, shall this glorious age begin, and the mighty months commence their march; under your sway any lingering traces of our guilt shall become void and release the earth from its continual dread. He shall have the gift of divine life, shall see heroes mingled with gods, and shall himself be seen by them, and shall rule the world to which his father's prowess brought peace.

[18] But for you, child, the earth untilled will pour forth its first pretty gifts, gadding ivy with foxglove everywhere, and the Egyptian bean blended with the laughing briar; unbidden it will pour forth for you a cradle of smiling flowers. Unbidden, the goats will bring home their udders swollen with milk, and the cattle will not fear huge lions. The serpent, too, will perish, and perish will the plant that hides its poison; Assyrian spice will spring up on every soil.

[26] But as soon as you can read of the glories of heroes and your father's deeds, and can know what valour is, slowly will the plains yellow with the waving corn, on wild brambles the purple grape will hang, and the stubborn oak distil dewy honey.

[31] Yet will a few traces of old-time sin live on, to bid men tempt the sea in ships, girdle towns with walls, and cleave the earth with furrows. A second Tiphys will then arise, and a second Argo to carry chosen heroes; a second war will be fought, and great Achilles be sent again to Troy.

[37] Next, when now the strength of years has made you a man, even the trader will quit the sea, nor will the ship of pine exchange wares; every land will bear all fruits. Earth will not suffer the harrow, nor the vine the pruning hook; the sturdy ploughman, too, will now loose his oxen from the yoke. No more will wool be taught to put on varied hues, but of himself the ram in the meadows will change his fleece, now to sweetly blushing purple, now to a saffron yellow; and scarlet shall clothe the grazing lambs at will.

[46] "Ages so blessed, glide on!" cried the Fates to their spindles, voicing in unison the fixed will of Destiny.

[48] O enter upon your high honours – the hour will soon be here – dear offspring of the gods, mighty seed of a Jupiter to be! See how the world bows with its massive dome – earth and expanse of sea and heaven's depth! See how all things rejoice in the age that is at hand!

[53] I pray that the twilight of a long life may then be vouchsafed me, and inspiration enough to hymn your deeds! Then shall neither Thracian Orpheus

nor Linus vanquish me in song, though mother give aid to the one and father to the other, Calliope to Orpheus, to Linus fair Apollo. Even were Pan to compete with me and Arcady be judge, then even Pan, with Arcady for judge, would own himself defeated.

[60] Begin, baby boy, to recognize your mother with a smile: ten months have brought your mother long travail. Begin, baby boy! The child who has not won a smile from his parents, no god ever honoured with his table, no goddess with her bed!

APPENDIX II

HORACE : *CARMEN SAECULARE*

Phoebe silvarumque potens Diana,
lucidum caeli decus, o colendi
semper et culti, date quae precamur
    tempore sacro,

quo Sibyllini monuere versus   *[5]*
virgines lectas puerosque castos
dis, quibus septem placuere colles,
    dicere carmen.

alme Sol, curru nitido diem qui
promis et celas aliusque et idem   *[10]*
nasceris, possis nihil urbe Roma
    visere maius.

Rite maturos aperire partus
lenis, Ilithyia, tuere matres,
sive tu Lucina probas vocari   *[15]*
    seu Genitalis:

diva, producas subolem patrumque
prosperes decreta super iugandis
feminis prolisque novae feraci
    lege marita,   *[20]*

certus undenos deciens per annos
orbis ut cantus referatque ludos
ter die claro totiensque grata
    nocte frequentis.

Vosque, veraces cecinisse Parcae,   *[25]*
quod semel dictum est stabilisque rerum
terminus servet, bona iam peractis
    iungite fata.

fertilis frugum pecorisque Tellus
spicea donet Cererem corona;   *[30]*
nutriant fetus et aquae salubres
    et Iovis aurae.

condito mitis placidusque telo
supplices audi pueros, Apollo;
siderum regina bicornis, audi,   [35]
    Luna, puellas.

Roma si vestrum est opus Iliaeque
litus Etruscum tenuere turmae,
iussa pars mutare lares et urbem
    sospite cursu,   [40]

cui per ardentem sine fraude Troiam
castus Aeneas patriae superstes
liberum munivit iter, daturus
    plura relictis:

di, probos mores docili iuventae,   [45]
di, senectuti placidae quietem,
Romulae genti date remque prolemque
    et decus omne.

Quaeque vos bobus veneratur albis
clarus Anchisae Venerisque sanguis,   [50]
impetret, bellante prior, iacentem
    lenis in hostem.

iam mari terraque manus potentis
Medus Albanasque timet securis,
iam Scythae responsa petunt, superbi   [55]
    nuper et Indi.

iam Fides et Pax et Honos Pudorque
priscus et neglecta redire Virtus
audet adparetque beata pleno
    Copia cornu.   [60]

Augur et fulgente decorus arcu
Phoebus acceptusque novem Camenis,
qui salutari levat arte fessos
    corporis artus,

si Palatinas videt aequos aras,   [65]
remque Romanam Latiumque felix
alterum in lustrum meliusque semper
    prorogat aevum,

quaeque Aventinum tenet Algidumque,
quindecim Diana preces virorum   *[70]*
curat et votis puerorum amicas
    adplicat auris.

Haec Iovem sentire deosque cunctos
spem bonam certamque domum reporto,
doctus et Phoebi chorus et Dianae   *[75]*
    dicere laudes.

From Horace: The Epodes and *Carmen Saeculare* by Horace and A. S. Kline (translator),

Copyright © 2005

O Phoebus, Diana queen of the woodlands,
Bright heavenly glories, both worshipped forever
And cherished forever, now grant what we pray for
At this sacred time,

When Sybilline verses have issued their warning   [5]
To innocent boys, and the virgins we've chosen,
To sing out their song to the gods, who have shown their
Love for the Seven Hills.

O kindly Sun, in your shining chariot, who
Heralds the day, then hides it, to be born again   [10]
New yet the same, you will never know anything
Mightier than Rome!

O gentle Ilithyia, duly revealing
The child at full term, now protect gentle mothers,
Whether you'd rather be known as Lucina,   [15]
Or Genitalis.

Goddess, nurture our offspring, bring to fruition
The Senate's decrees concerning the wedlock
Of women who'll bear us more of our children,
The laws of marriage,   [20]

So the fixed cycle of years, ten times eleven,
Will bring back the singing again, bring back the games
We crowd to three times by daylight, as often,
By beautiful night.

And you, the Fates, who are truthful in prophecy,   [25]
Link happy destinies, as has once been ordained
And let the certain course of events confirm it,
To those that are past.

Let Earth that is fruitful in crops, and in cattle,
Adorn our Ceres with garlands of wheat-ears: [30]
And may Jupiter's life-giving rain and breezes
Ripen the harvest.

Gentle and peaceful Apollo, lay down your arms,
And listen now to the young lads' supplications:
Luna, crescent-horned queen of the constellations, [35]
Give ear to the girls.

If Rome is your doing, and if from far Ilium
Came that band of people who reached the Tuscan shore,
Those commanded to change their home and their city,
On a lucky course,   [40]

Those for whom pious Aeneas, the survivor,
Who passed without injury through the flames of Troy,
Prepared a path to freedom, destined to grant him
Much more than he'd lost:

Then, you divinities, show our receptive youth   [45]
Virtue, grant peace and quiet to the old, and give
Children and wealth to the people of Romulus,
And every glory.

Whatever a noble descendant of Venus
And Anchises, asks, with a white steer's sacrifice, [50]
Let him obtain: a winner in war, merciful
To our fallen foe.

Now the Parthians fear our forces, powerful
On land, and on sea: they fear the Alban axes,
Now the once proud Indians, now the Scythians   [55]
Beg for an answer.

Now Faith and Peace, Honour, and ancient Modesty,
Dare to return once more, with neglected Virtue,
And blessed Plenty dares to appear again, now,
With her flowing horn.   [60]

May Phoebus, the augur, decked with the shining bow,
Phoebus who's dear to the Nine Muses, that Phoebus
Who can offer relief to a weary body
With his healing art,

May he, if he favours the Palatine altars,   [65]
Extend Rome's power, and Latium's good-fortune,
Through the fresh ages, show, always, improvement,
Lustra ever new.

And may Diana, to whom is the Aventine,
And Mount Algidus, accept the entreaties   [70]
Of the Fifteen, and attend, and lend a fond ear,
To these children's prayers.

We bear to our home the fine hope, and certain,
That such is Jupiter's, and all the gods' purpose:
We're taught, we, the chorus, to sing praise of Phoebus,   [75]
Praise of Diana.

APPENDIX III

Extract from Ovid: Metamorphoses Book I

Aurea prima sata est aetas, quae vindice nullo,
sponte sua, sine lege fidem rectumque colebat.   *[90]*
poena metusque aberant, nec verba minantia fixo
aere legebantur, nec supplex turba timebat
iudicis ora sui, sed erant sine vindice tuti.
nondum caesa suis, peregrinum ut viseret orbem,
montibus in liquidas pinus descenderat undas,   *[95]*
nullaque mortales praeter sua litora norant;
nondum praecipites cingebant oppida fossae;
non tuba derecti, non aeris cornua flexi,
non galeae, non ensis erat: sine militis usu
mollia securae peragebant otia gentes.   *[100]*
ipsa quoque inmunis rastroque intacta nec ullis
saucia vomeribus per se dabat omnia tellus,
contentique cibis nullo cogente creatis
arbuteos fetus montanaque fraga legebant
cornaque et in duris haerentia mora rubetis   *[105]*
et quae deciderant patula Iovis arbore glandes.
ver erat aeternum, placidique tepentibus auris
mulcebant zephyri natos sine semine flores;
mox etiam fruges tellus inarata ferebat,
nec renovatus ager gravidis canebat aristis;   *[110]*
flumina iam lactis, iam flumina nectaris ibant,
flavaque de viridi stillabant ilice mella.

    Postquam Saturno tenebrosa in Tartara misso
sub Iove mundus erat, subiit argentea proles,
auro deterior, fulvo pretiosior aere.   *[115]*
Iuppiter antiqui contraxit tempora veris
perque hiemes aestusque et inaequalis autumnos
et breve ver spatiis exegit quattuor annum.
tum primum siccis aer fervoribus ustus
canduit, et ventis glacies adstricta pependit;   *[120]*
tum primum subiere domos; domus antra fuerunt
et densi frutices et vinctae cortice virgae.
semina tum primum longis Cerealia sulcis
obruta sunt, pressique iugo gemuere iuvenci.

Tertia post illam successit aenea proles,   *[125]*
saevior ingeniis et ad horrida promptior arma,
non scelerata tamen; de duro est ultima ferro.
protinus inrupit venae peioris in aevum
omne nefas: fugere pudor verumque fidesque;
in quorum subiere locum fraudesque dolusque   *[130]*
insidiaeque et vis et amor sceleratus habendi.
vela dabant ventis nec adhuc bene noverat illos
navita, quaeque prius steterant in montibus altis,
fluctibus ignotis insultavere carinae,
communemque prius ceu lumina solis et auras   *[135]*
cautus humum longo signavit limite mensor.
nec tantum segetes alimentaque debita dives
poscebatur humus, sed itum est in viscera terrae,
quasque recondiderat Stygiisque admoverat umbris,
effodiuntur opes, inritamenta malorum.   *[140]*
iamque nocens ferrum ferroque nocentius aurum
prodierat, prodit bellum, quod pugnat utroque,
sanguineaque manu crepitantia concutit arma.
vivitur ex rapto: non hospes ab hospite tutus,
non socer a genero, fratrum quoque gratia rara est;   *[145]*
inminet exitio vir coniugis, illa mariti,
lurida terribiles miscent aconita novercae,
filius ante diem patrios inquirit in annos:
victa iacet pietas, et virgo caede madentis
ultima caelestum terras Astraea reliquit.   *[150]*

OVID, VOL. III, translated by Frank Justus Miller, Loeb Classical Library Volume 42, Cambridge Mass.: Harvard University Press, First published 1917. Loeb Clasical Library ® is a registered trademark of the President and Fellows of Harvard College.

Golden was that first age, which, with no one to compel, without a law of its own will, kept faith and did the right. There was no fear of punishment, no threatening words were to be read on brazen tablets; no suppliant throng gazed fearfully upon its judge's face; but without judges, lived secure. Not yet had the pine-tree, felled on its native mountains, descended thence into the watery plain to visit other lands; men knew no shores except their own. Not yet were cities begirt with steep moats; there were no trumpets of straight, no horns of curving brass, no swords or helmets. There was no need at all of armed men, for nations, secure from war's alarms, passed the years in gentle ease. The earth herself, without compulsion, untouched by hoe or plowshare, of herself gave all things needful. And men, content with food which came with no one's seeking, gathered the arbute fruit, strawberries from the mountain-sides cornel-cherries, berries hanging thick upon the prickly bramble, and acorns, fallen from the spreading tree of Jove. Then spring was everlasting, and gentle zephyrs with warm breath played with the flowers that sprang unplanted. Anon the earth, untilled, brought forth her stores of grain, and the fields, though unfallowed, grew white with the heavy, bearded wheat. Streams of milk and streams of sweet nectar flowed, and yellow honey was distilled from the verdant oak.

After Saturn had been banished to the dark land of death, and the world was under the sway of Jove the **Silver** race came in, lower in the scale than gold, but of greater worth than yellow brass. Jove now shortened the bounds of the old-time spring, and through winter, summer, variable autumn, and brief spring completed the year in four seasons. Then first the parched air glared white with burning heat, and icicles hung down congealed by freezing winds. In that age men first sought the shelter of houses. Their homes had heretofore been caves, dense thickets, and branches bound together with bark. Then first the seeds of grain were planted in long furrows, and bullocks groaned beneath the heavy yoke.

Next after this and third in order came the **Brazen** race, of sterner disposition, and more ready to fly to arms savage, but not yet impious. The age of hard **Iron** came last. Straightway all evil burst forth into this age of baser vein: modesty and truth and faith fled the earth, and in their place came tricks and plots and snares, violence and cursed love of gain as yet scarce knew them; and keels of pine which long had stood upon high mountain-sides, now leaped insolently over unknown waves. And the ground, which had hitherto been a common possession like the sunlight and the air, the careful surveyor now marked out with long-drawn boundary-line. Not only did men demand of the bounteous fields the crops and sustenance they owed, but they delved as well into the very bowels of the earth; and the wealth which the creator had hidden away and buried deep amidst the very Stygian shades, was brought to light, wealth that pricks men on to crime. And now baneful iron had come, and gold more baneful than iron; war came, which fights with both, and bran dished in its bloody hands the clashing arms. Men lived on plunder. Guest was not safe from host, nor father-in-law from son-in-law; even among brothers 'twas rare to find affection. The husband longed for the death of his wife, she of her husband; murderous stepmothers brewed deadly poisons, and sons inquired into their fathers' years before the time. Piety lay vanquished, and the maiden Astraea, last of the immortals, abandoned the blood-soaked earth.

APPENDIX IV

AN IMAGINED EYEWITNESS ACCOUNT OF THE SAECULAR GAMES OF AD 204

Introduction

An imagined account of the Saecular Games of Septimius Severus constructed from the Severan commentarii.[783] *This is an attempt to describe the key events of AD 204 and where the details are missing from the Severan account, the records from the Saecular Games of Augustus and Domitian have been used to fill gaps and some further details are speculative.*

Preparatory Ceremonies 23rd May AD 204

For several months, official heralds, in plumed helmets and ancient ceremonial dress, had made dramatic announcements in the Forum at Rome, and in major cities.[784] They proclaimed that, following a Sybilline prophecy,[785] the seventh Saecular Games [786] would shortly be held in Rome and would mark the phenomenal start of a new era. This was the start of new Golden Age and would be commemorated with events and rituals so sensational they had never been seen before nor would they ever be seen again in their lifetime. [787]

The High Council of Fifteen Officials for Sacred Services, chaired by the Emperor Septimius Severus, had also issued proclamations which specified the dates of ceremonies to prepare for the three days and nights of sacred rituals; if the auspices were favourable, these would be followed by a spectacular series of games and entertainment for which no expense would be spared.

On the first appointed day, 23rd May AD 204, crowds gathered at the Temple of Palatine Apollo, the magnificent temple which had been built by Augustus himself over 200 years before. They were directed to a huge colonnaded precinct [788] which overlooked the Circus Maximus and the rooftops of Rome. A special ceremonial platform had been set up upon which the Council of Fifteen, including

---

783 Pighi, 1941, 137-175; CIL VI 32326-32335; Rantala, 2017, 172-190.

784 A tombstone in Rome records the death of a man from Tripolis who travelled to attend the Saecular Games: *Corpus Inscriptionum Graecarum* 5921.2.

785 Pighi, 1941, 142.

786 Censorinus states that the Severan Games were the eighth (Censorinus, *De Die Natali*, XVII. 29) but there are numerous references in the Severan *Commentarii* which declare them to be the seventh Games (CIL VI 32326-32335).

787 Herodian, 3.6.10; see Rowan, 2012, 50 -51;

788 Wiseman, 2019, 109; Carandini, 2017, 234.

the Emperor himself and the Crown Prince, were grandly seated in readiness for this ancient public ceremony. Every member of the Council was finely dressed in fringed, purple ceremonial robes magnificently embroidered for the occasion.

The Director of the preparations for the Saecular Games, Pompeius Rusonianus, rose to his feet. He declared that, by an official decree of the Council of Fifteen, headed by the Emperor, whose names and titles he recited, the City of Rome had to be ritually purified for seven consecutive days before the Saecular Games could begin.[789] He declared the sacred places where the purificatory materials were to be distributed would now be drawn by lot. An official came forward with the ritual bowl and members of the Council took it in turns to draw lots from the bowl. As each lot was drawn a secretary read out the name of the location and a scribe recorded the sacred locations where the incense, sulphur, bitumen, and torches would be given out that evening.[790]

Once all the lots had been drawn, Pompeius Rusonianus stood to make a further declaration. He announced that the seventh official Saecular games in the history of the Empire would be celebrated shortly and that there should be general rejoicing of all people. The Director declared that all prosecutions would be suspended for thirty days. All property owners in cities and in rural areas were urged to be mindful of security during the Games. He declared that costly incense for burning at household shrines and other purificatory materials would be distributed in Rome the following day at the temple of Palatine Apollo. He further declared that, in two days time, the ancient ceremony of the giving of first fruits to the Council of Fifteen would take place at four temples: the temple of Palatine Apollo, the temple of Capitoline Jupiter, the neighbouring temple of Jupiter the Thunderer and the Temple of Diana on the Aventine Hill.[791] These food offerings mainly consisted of wheat, barley and beans[792] which echoed a mythical ritual of Romulus at the founding of Rome[793] and which were also symbolic of the fertility of the new Golden Age.

First Night Rituals, 31st May AD 204

The first events took place at night in front of the temples to Dis and Proserpina, deities of the underworld. These temples were in the Campus Martius,[794] by the river Tiber in an area known as the Tarentum. To one side of the temples a magnificent new marble monument had been recently built by the Emperor and depicted scenes from myths of Hercules and Bacchus, the patron deities of

---

789 Pighi, 1941, 146.

790 Forsythe, 2012,73. ILS 5050A.

791 Augustan *Commentarii* (CIL 32323-4) lists four locations in front of four temples: Capitoline temple of Jupiter, the neighbouring temple Jupiter the thunderer (*Iovis Tonantis*), the temple of Palatine Apollo and the temple of Diana on the Aventine.

792 Zosimus, 2.4.3.

793 Plutarch, Life of Romulus. 11; Ovid *Fasti* IV.819; Forsyth, 2012,75; Romulus put first fruits into a circular trench.

794 The Campus Martius was known as 'a place of rebirth': Rantala, 2017, 57.

these Saecular Games.[795] Once everyone was assembled, the Emperor made a ceremonial entry accompanied by priests and attendants for the ritual sacrifices. Roman priests normally carried out sacrifices with a veiled head (*capite velato*) but at the Saecular Games the rituals followed the Greek or Etruscan practice of the head being uncovered except for a coronet of laurel leaves.

Imperial musicians played an ancient Greek hymn on a Greek double flute (*aulos*) and lyre (*cithara*). Nine ewes and nine she-goats, all black in colour, were then brought forward to be prepared for sacrifice according to ancient Greek ritual. Grains of wheat and drops of water were sprinkled on the animals' heads and a few tufts of hair were cut from brow of each animal and burnt on the altar as an act of consecration.

At this point the Emperor, Septimius Severus, stepped forward, head uncovered, for the opening prayer in front of the ancient altars. In convoluted, ancient words and phrases, the Emperor invoked the mysterious triple Greek goddesses of Fate, the *Moirae*, and announced the sacrifices as set down in the Sybilline books. He entreated the Fates, just as they had increased the might and majesty of the Roman Empire, to bestow everlasting peace and health to all Roman citizens and to keep them safe and secure. The Emperor called on these powerful, ancient goddesses of Destiny to show favour to the People of Rome, to the Council of Fifteen and to the Emperor's family and household.

The sacrificial knife was then put to work and the pungent smell of fresh blood filled the air. Once the entrails had been inspected by the *haruspex* the flesh was placed in a sacred ditch and burnt as an offering to the gods of the underworld. [796]

When the rituals were complete, the spectators were invited to move to an area nearby where a stage had been set up. There was no seating and no scenery on the wooden stage – just a shimmering dark blue curtain suspended at the back of the stage as a backdrop. In front of this curtain a mime actor would perform a sacred drama. He wore a full-length white silk tunic and his face was covered by a Greek mask which emphasised his large expressive eyes. He used his sinuous arms and hands, which were painted white, to express a whole range of emotions.[797] The sacred drama was played out using exotic ancient mime and dance which portrayed the myth of the origin and location of the Saecular Games.[798] This was quite unlike the presentation of any contemporary plays seen at Rome. Using incredibly athletic movement and simple props, such as a flowing silk scarf, the story of the ancient myth was vividly acted out

---

795 The remnants are fragmentary and interpretation is hypothetical; Gorrie, 2002, 461; Rowan, 2012, 59.

796 Rupke, 2011, 266; The *haruspex* was a type of augur or official diviner; see Santangelo, 2013, 84-114.

797 Zanobi, 2008, 15.

798 Rantala, 2017, 143.

by the mime artist. Music from flutes, lyres and percussion with an offstage chorus of singers heightened the drama.

Figure 164: Roman mime mask, 1st or 2nd century AD, © British Museum 1873,0820.568

The mime told the story of a Sabine man, Valesius,[799] whose house and trees had been struck by lightning – a bad omen from the gods. His three children became severely ill. The augurs told him to travel to Tarentum which he thought was to be found in Apulia. On his way there he stopped by the Tibur in an area which bore the same name as the Spartan colony in the south of the country – the Tarentum. The children were miraculously cured. They told their father of a dream in which the gods ordered that a sacrifice of black animals be made to Dis and Proserpina over three nights and days on an underground altar. Valesius wanted to give thanks for the restored health of his three children and, by another miracle, Valesius's servant discovered an ancient buried altar which was appropriate to carry out the wishes of the gods.

Guided by the torchlight, the spectators then walked to the Temple of *Concordia* in the Forum where more crowds were gathering. To one side stood the Temple of Saturn under whose traditional auspices the new age was being ushered in. Directly opposite was the newly completed and splendid Arch of Septimius Severus celebrating his victory against the Parthians. On the top of the monument were life size statues of the imperial family smiling down benignly on the birth of a new Severan era for Rome.

The forecourt of the ancient temple was the setting for a magnificent ritual banquet – known as a *sellisternium* - for the goddesses Juno and Diana with 110 matrons, led by the Empress Julia Domna, all dressed in their finest silks and glittering jewelry. The ritual banquet celebrated the concord between gods

---

799 The subject of the mime is speculation but based on a key foundation myth: Zosimus, *Historia Nova*, Book 2. See also: Valerius Maximus, Memorable Doings and Sayings, II.4.5.

and mankind, hence the setting. The table was lit by a series of colossal antique bronze candelabra dating back to Augustan times. Two additional places at the table were set for the goddesses Juno and Diana, represented by their attributes of a peacock and a crown for Juno and triple crescent moons for Diana, set upon oversize, elaborately draped, ceremonial chairs.

*Figure 165: Draped ceremonial chair (Sella) on a marble frieze from Ravenna ©
G Barker*

As was the custom, the waiters then distributed the food through the City to share the sacred meal with the whole community. Doors of houses were left open and food and wine was shared with everyone including visitors to the city, those in mourning and even accused prisoners who had been released from their cells for the duration of the ceremonies.[800]

First Day and Second Night Rituals 1ˢᵗ June AD 204

The following afternoon crowds gathered on the Capitoline Hill for the next sacred ritual which was to be celebrated in front the altar of the temple of Jupiter, Best and Greatest of the gods. Once again, the Council of Fifteen were gathered in their ceremonial robes. The sound of the Greek double flute and lyre filled the air and three magnificent white bulls, their heads lowered by means of a harness, were led forward by officials. Grains and water were duly sprinkled on their brows and tufts of hair burned on the great altar. The Emperor, wearing a coronet of laurel leaves, stepped forward to recite the prayer in ancient phrases. This was similar in format to the prayer offered to the fates, known by the Greek name of the *Moirae*, but this time it was addressed to Jupiter, Best and

---

800 Livy, History, V 13. 5-8; Livy describes the first *Lectisternium* in Rome. The possible development
of the *Sellisternium* is discussed by Beer, 2011, 11 -15.

Greatest. The Emperor recited the prayer and each bull, having been stunned, was sacrificed with one tremendous swinging blow from the sacred axe.

That night, there was a further ritual at the Tarentum. This time a sacrifice was offered to Eileithyia, the Greek goddess of childbirth, known to Romans as Lucina. This was not a blood sacrifice but three batches of nine specially baked cakes which were burnt as an offering. A further sacred drama was enacted this time in an enormous wooden theatre. This drama was more conventional in style, with no masks, and included splendid scenery and costumes. The play was about the origins of Rome and the central importance of the goddess Vesta. [801] Those performing in this drama included leading priestesses from the sacred Vestal Virgin community Numisia, Maximilla and Terentia Flavola.[802] This was followed by another ritual banquet or *Sellisternium* in honour of Juno and Diana which was just as magnificent as that of the first night.

Figure 166: Matrons at a Sellisternium from the Claudian 'Ara Pietatis'[803] Museo del Ara Pacis, Rome © G Barker

Second Day and Night Rituals 2ⁿᵈ June AD 204

On the afternoon of the second day, the altar in front of the Temple of Jupiter on the Capitoline Hill, was the setting for a sacrifice of two white cows to Juno, Queen of Heaven. This time, the younger son of the Emperor, Geta Caesar, also took part in performing the ritual alongside the High Council of Fifteen Officials. This was followed by the sacrifice of a white bull to Jupiter Best and Greatest. Now the central doors of the temple were open to reveal the

---

801 The subject of the sacred drama is speculative but seems likely given the number of times the Vestals are mentioned in the Severan *Commentarii*. See Rantala, 2017, 120.

802 Pighi, 1941,157.

803 There is a possibility that the fragments of the so-called *Ara Pietatis* may in fact represent a record of the Claudian *Ludi Saeculares*.

statue of Jupiter. The Emperor and members of the Council of Fifteen with invited guests then processed to the Palatine where Septimius Severus hosted a magnificent banquet.

After the banquet, the party returned to the Temple of Jupiter, Best and Greatest, where the decorated cult statue of Juno Queen of Heaven was once again revealed. An invocation to Juno on bended knee was made by 110 Matrons, led by the Empress, Julia Domna and the senior Vestal Virgins. They prayed for eternal security, victory, for the good health for Rome, all its citizens and the legions of Rome. They prayed that Rome and its citizens would be kept from harm, be made stronger and that Juno, Queen of Heaven, would show favour to all Roman citizens and especially to all those present, the Council of Fifteen and all households and families.

Following this invocation, the Emperor and his party processed to the magnificent wooden theatre, specially constructed on the Campus Martius, where the Emperor made an announcement. He declared, to tumultuous applause, that following the proper observance of three days and nights of rituals, seven days of the Honorary Games would be held at public expense. Grand theatrical performances and drama contests would be presented in not one but three theatres: the vast wooden theatre, specially constructed for the occasion, the theatre of Pompey and the Odeon. These venues would feature extravagant, productions of the famous pantomimes of Pylades, Apolaustus and Marcus. Spectacular circus feats on horseback would be seen in the Circus Maximus. The same venue would then stage seven major chariot races, with chariots drawn by four horses. There was serious prize money for the victors and the amounts for each winner were announced. Following the races, animal hunts with the most exotic and dangerous animals would be staged. This would be such a dangerous display that special safety measures were announced to ensure the security of the spectators and all those who attended were strongly advised to follow safety instructions. In the arena there would be displayed no less than 100 of each of the following seven types of exotic animals: lions, lionesses, leopards, bears, bison, wild asses and ostriches.

That night, a key sacrifice took place at the Tarentum but this time dedicated to Terra Mater, known to Romans as Tellus or Mother Earth. Firstly, a sacrifice of incense and wine was made by the Emperor and the ceremonial knife was ritually purified. A pregnant sow was then offered in sacrifice following the Greek rite. The flesh was ritually burnt in a pit by the altar and dedicated to Mother Earth.

Figure 167: Sestertius of Caracalla with reverse showing sacrifice of sow to Terra Mater with the Patron gods, Hercules and Bacchus, RIC IV 761 var © Private collection

This sacrifice was followed by further spectacular theatre performances. Finally, another Sellisternium or sacred banquet to Juno and Diana, just as extravagant as the last, was held in front of the Temple of *Concordia*.

Third Day Rituals – 3rd June AD 204

The start of the third day of rituals took place at the Temple of Palatine Apollo which had been the scene of the first ceremony 10 days before. The Emperor offered a sacrifice of 27 cakes to Apollo and Diana and then announced the final ritual. This would be the performance of the *Carmen Saeculare* or Saecular Hymn to mark the start of a new era of peace and prosperity. This had been specially commissioned for the occasion and would be performed as a choral dance[804] by 27 boys and 27 girls with living parents.[805]

The Imperial family and the Council of Fifteen in their richly decorated ceremonial robes were escorted by heralds to their chairs on the platform before the Temple of Apollo. Then all the girls and boys, carrying laurel branches in honour of Apollo, took their positions in front of imperial platform with boys one side and girls on the other. All the girls were dressed in white silk and the boys in imperial purple. [806]

Accompanied by imperial musicians playing Greek instruments, the children sang of Apollo and Diana who were invoked to listen to the prayers of the Saecular Games. The music for the hymn had been specially composed in the style of an ancient Greek paean to Apollo which lent an air of holy antiquity to the performance. [807] As they sang, the children performed a solemn dance moving in carefully choreographed circles.

---

804 Pighi, 1941, 167; Rantala, 2017, 189.

805 Thomas, R. ed. (2011), 54.

806 Statius, *Silvae*,1.4.96-97: Not for nothing did you boys, dressed in patrician purple, lately sound your song in my honour; *neque enim frustra mihi super honors carmina Patricio, pueri, sonuistis in ostro*.

807 Hijmans, 2009, 562.

Figure 168: Aureus of Septimius Severus showing Felicitas/Tellus with three boys and three girls©Vienna Kunsthistorisches Museum: RÖ 1446

They sang about the sacred saecular period of 110 years foretold by Sybilline prophecy. [808] They sang of the good fortune of new Golden Age making the earth fruitful in crops and cattle; they sang of ships sailing to the distant cities and shores of the Roman Empire and they sang of the Virtue of Hercules and the Golden Fields of Bacchus.[809] The boys again invoked the power of Palatine Apollo and the girls prayed for Diana's protection for the birth of the new *saeculum*. The final verses invoked the gods' protection for all leaders of men appointed by the gods in the new Golden Age.

The Director of the Games, then instructed the children to lead a state procession along the *Via Sacra* in the Forum to the temple of Jupiter on the Capitoline Hill. Each boy and girl paired off and held hands while they processed, still holding the laurel branches. As well as the imperial family and the High Council of Fifteen officials, the procession was joined by musicians, including horn players and trumpeters. Also processing were actors and mime artists from the stage shows who leapt and waved to the crowds, the many attendants from the various arenas, the heralds, two and four horse racing teams, acrobats and circus riders who performed somersaults and other tricks for the crowds as they processed. [810] The long procession snaked its way along the sacred road in the Forum and passed under the new triumphal arch of Septimius Severus, the first to be built in the Forum for two centuries. [811]

Once everyone had assembled in front of the temple of Jupiter, the boys and girls gave a repeat performance of the Saecular Hymn. That evening a final sacred banquet was held before the Temple of *Concordia*.

The Honorary Games

As announced by the Emperor, there followed seven days of games and celebratory entertainments. Drama competitions amongst the famous writers

---

808 Horace, Carmen Saeculare, line 21; as the Severan games were held 220 years after the Augustan Games it is reasonable to assume the period of 110 years was mentioned in the Severan *Carmen*.

809 Pighi, 1941,165; Rantala, 2017, 189.

810 Pighi, 1941, 166; Rantala, 2017, 189.

811 Gorrie, 2004, 88.

and actors of the day were staged in the largest theatres Rome had to offer. Theatrical spectacles also included classic and rarely performed mimes and drama by writers from the time of Augustus. These were put on at the Theatre of Pompey which had been splendidly restored by the Emperor,[812] at the Odeon and at the spectacular wooden theatre on the Campus Martius. Horse races, featuring the most famous charioteers of the day, in the Circus Maximus brought enormous crowds to their feet shouting for their favourite colour team to win.

The Circus had a huge ship's sail at its centre. This was a reference to the ships sailing to the edges of the Empire which had been sung about in the *Carmen Saeculare*. No less than seven races were staged to reflect the fact that these were the seventh Saecular Games. Each race represented the cyclical nature of the *saecula* which brought back the returning Golden Age. [813] Huge sums of money were on offer to the victorious winner of each race. In between the races trick riders performed seemingly impossible acrobatics while riding at speed round the Circus.

Figure 169: Quadriga race in mosaic from Piazza Armerina© G Barker

A monumental ship was also built for the hunting Games in the Colosseum. Parts of this ship were designed to split from the rest of the structure from which emerged various types of exotic animals ostriches, lions and lionesses, wild asses, bears, leopards and bison. Seven types of animal had been chosen to reflect the seventh Saecular Games. Then the professional hunters both mounted and on foot entered the arena and put on an expert display of hunting the various animals.

812 Gorrie, 2002, 461.
813 Abdy, 2019, 38.

Figure 170: Aureus of Septimius Severus showing ships with animals and quadrigae (RIC IV 274) © Roma Numismatics Auction 4, Lot 574, September 2012 https://www.romanumismatics.com

The climax of the seven day spectacle was the Trojan War Games which were staged at the Circus Maximus.[814] This was an exciting though dangerous set of manoeuvres performed by boys on horseback from patrician families who were under the age of 13. Great skills of horsemanship were required. Like many aspects of the Saecular Games, the Trojan War Games had a purificatory function. As described by the great poet Virgil, they were of ancient origin and originally formed part of the funeral games of Anchises.[815] This was a fitting climax to the Saecular Games which also celebrated the mythical Trojan origins of Rome.

There were forty-five boys taking part. All carried two lances with iron tips and sported a torque of twisted gold round their necks. For the early manoeuvres the boys wore a garland of leaves on their heads though later they donned helmets and breastplates. [816]

At the crack of a whip, the forty-five riders cantered forward in one perfect formation. At the next crack of the whip they divided into three teams of fifteen with each leader bearing a Trojan name: Priam, Atys and Iulus.

The patterns in which the three groups rode became progressively more complicated with different groups riding across each other with perfect precision. The circular patterns in which they rode required firm handling of the horses. At a given moment, the horses would sometimes leap in the air like dolphins which the crowd applauded. At first, the pace was steady but gradually the speed increased and one mistake could lead to serious injury for horse or rider; as the riding became more dangerous so the boys started whooping and shouting war cries.

814 Suetonius, Nero, 7.

815 Virgil, *Aeneid*, Book V, 545-603; for a possible Etruscan link to the *Lusus Troiae*: see Bell, 2013, 4172.

816 Burgersdijk (2012) 90.

Figure 171: Sestertius of Nero which may depict the Trojan War Games[817] RIC1 436 © British Museum R.10034

At the end of the display, all riders lined up in their three teams and saluted the Emperor to rapturous applause from the vast crowd. The boys then dismounted and were presented, one by one, to the Emperor who gave each of the principal riders a specially engraved silver salver.[818]

The closing ceremony of the Saecular Games took place that evening at the Tarentum in the vast wooden theatre. The rituals and games were pronounced to have been successfully conducted and thanks were given to the Director of the Games and all those who had been responsible for organising the series of spectacular events, especially the Council of Fifteen. Further thanks were given to all participants and especially to all the children who performed the Saecular Hymn. A final prayer was offered to all the relevant gods and goddesses of the Saecular Games as well as the patron deities chosen by the Emperor. After the success of these spectacular Games it seemed as though a new era of peace and prosperity had truly begun, under the rightful rule of the Emperor Septimius Severus, the new Augustus, and his dynasty as ordained by Sybilline prophecy and the stars themselves.

817 Smith, 2000, 282-289.For Nero's obsession with the *Lusus Troiae* see: Suetonius, Nero, 10.2; Cassius Dio 62.29.1; Suetonius uses the term *decvrsio* to describe the Trojan War games: Suetonius, Gaius, 18.

818 Pighi, 2041, 167; Rantala, 2017, 189.

Bibliography of Primary Sources

Apuleius, *Metamorphoses (or The Golden Ass)*.
Augustus, court of, *Res Gestae Divi Augustus*.
Aratus, *Phaenomena*.
Arnobius, *Adversus Gentes; Adversus Nationes*.
Cassiodorus, *Chronica*.
Cassius Dio, *Historia Romana*.
Censorinus, *De Die Natali*.
Cicero, *De Natura Deorum*; *De Imperio*.
Claudian, *Collected works*.
Eumenius, *Panegyrici Latini*.
Eutropius, *Breviarum*.
Eusebius, *Historia Ecclesiastica; Praeparatio Evangelica*.
Herodotus, *The Histories of Herodotus*.
Herodian, *Historia Augusta*.
Hesiod, *Works and Days*.
Homer, *The Iliad*.
Horace, *Carmen Saeculare*; *Epodes; Odes; Epistulae*.
Lactantius, *Divinae Institutiones*.
Malalas, *Chronicle*.
Martial, *Epigrams*.
Livy, *Historia Romana*.
Nonnus, *Dionysiaca*.
Orosius, *Historiarum Adversum Paganum*.
Ovid, *Fasti; Metamorphoses; Tristia*.
Philostratus, *Life of Apollonius*.
Plato, *The Statesman*; *Timaeus*.
Pliny, *Historia Naturalis*.
Plotinus, *The Enneads*.
Plutarch, *Lives of the Noble Greeks and Romans; Moralia*.
Porphyry, *Life of Plotin*us; The *Cave of the Nymphs*.
Scriptores Historiae Augustae.
Servius, *In Vergilii Aeneidem commentarii*.
Siculus, Calpurnius, *Bucolica*.
Siculus, Diodorus, *Bibliotecha Historica*.
Statius, Publius Papinius, *Silvae*.
Suetonius, *De Vita Caesarum*.
Tacitus, *Annales*.
Tertullian, *Apologia*; *De Resurrectione Mortuorum*.
Valerius Maximus, *Factorum et dictorum memorabilium*.
Varro, *De Re Rustica*.
Victor, Aurelius, *De Caesaribus*.
Virgil, *Aeneid*; *Eclogues; Georgics*.
Zonaras, *Epitome Historiarum*.
Zosimus, *Historia Nova*.

BIBLIOGRAPHY OF
SECONDARY SOURCES

Abdy, R. (2019) Roman Imperial Coinage, Volume II part 3. Spink.

Abdy, R. and Minnitt, S. (2002) 'Shapwick Villa', CHRB 10: 169-233.

Adam, R. (1764) Ruins of the Palace of the Emperor Diocletian. Scotland.

Adkins, L. and Adkins, R. (1996) Dictionary of Roman Religion. Oxford University Press.

Alföldi, A. (1929) 'The Numbering of the Victories of the Emperor Gallienus and of the Loyalty of his Legions', Numismatic Chronicle Vol. 9, no 35/36: 218-279.

(1997) 'From the Aion Plutonios of the Ptolemies to the *Saeculum Frugiferum* of the Roman Emperors' in *Redeunt Saturnia Regna*, eds. E. Alfoldi-Rosenbaum, S. Campbell, A. Easson, C. Arnold-Biuchi. Bonn: 135- 172.

Alföldi, M. (1958) '*Zum Lyoner Bleimedallion'*, Schweizer Münzblätter 8: 63-68.

Alföldy, G. (1975) *Krisen in der Antike:* Bewusstsein und Bewältigung. Dusselfdorf.

Amer, G. and Gawlikowski, M. (1985) '*Le Sanctuare impérial de Philippopolis,*' Damaszener Mitteilungen, 2: 1-15.

Anderson G. (1986) Philostratus: Biography and Belles Lettres in the Third Century AD. Routledge.

Ando, C. (2012) Imperial Rome AD 193 to 284: The Critical Century. Edinburgh University Press.

Anthony, V. and Abdy, R and Clewes, S. eds. (2019) The Beau Street, Bath hoard. Oxford: Archaeopress

Armstrong, D. (1987) 'Gallienus in Athens, 264', *Zeitschrift für Papyrologie und Epigraphik*, Bd. 70: 235-258.

Asolati, M. (2015) '*Flavio Costantino reggitore della ruota zodiacale'* in *Il Cielo in Terra ovvero della giusta distanza*, University of Padua Press: 189-200.

Balbuza, K. (2014) 'Virtues and Abstract Ideas Propagated by Marcia Otacilia Severa, Numismatic Evidence' in *Studies in Honour of Professor Maria Dzielska,* eds. K. Twardowska, M. Salamon, S. Sprawski, M. Stachura, S. Turlej. Kraków: 185-198.

Baldus, H.R. (1971) Uranius Antoninus: *Münzprägung und Geschichte*. Antiquitas III. Bonn.

Banchich, T. and Lane, L. (2009) The History of Zonaras from Alxander Severus to Theodosius the Great. Routledge.

Barker, D (1996) 'The Golden Age is proclaimed? The *Carmen Saeculare* and the renascence of the Golden Race.' The Classical Quarterly New Series, Vol 46 No.2: 434-446.

Barker, G. (2015) 'The Coinage of Carausius: Developing the Golden Age Ideology through the Saecular Games', Numismatic Chronicle, Vol. 175: 161-170.

Barker, R. (2001) Legitimating identities: the self representation of rulers and subjects. Cambridge University Press.

Barnes T, (2008) 'Aspects of the Severan Empire, Part 1: Severus as the New Augustus', New England Classical Journal, 35.4: 251-267.

Barton, T. (1994) Ancient Astrology. Routledge.

Bastien, P. (1959) '*Les émissions de l'atelier de Lyon en 293 et 294*' in Revue Numismatique, Vol. 6 No. 2 : 75-111.

Bastien, P., Amandry, M., Gautier, G. (1989) *Le Monnayage De L'Atelier de Lyon : 274-413 supplement, Le Medallion de Plomb de Lyon*. Wetteren.

Bastien, P. and Metzger, C. (1977) *Le Trésor de Beaurains (dit d'Arras)*. Numismatique Romaines X. Wetteren.

Beard, M. (1985) 'Writing and ritual: a study of diversity and expansion in the Arval acta', Papers of the British School at Rome Vol. 53: 114-162.

Beard, M., North, J., Price, S., (1998) Religions of Rome, Volume 2, A Sourcebook. Cambridge University Press.

Beck, R. (2006) The Religion of the Mithras Cult in the Roman Empire: Mysteries of the Unconquered Sun. Oxford University Press, 2006.

Beer, M. (2011) 'Guess who's coming to dinner? the origins and development of the *lectisternium*', Classical Association Annual Conference, Durham University.

Bell, S.W. (2013) '*Lusus Troiae*', Blackwell Encyclopedia of Ancient History, ed. R. Bagnall et al. Malden, Mass., Wiley-Blackwell.

Beresford, J. (1972) The Ancient Sailing Season. Brill.

Besley, E. and Bland, R. (1983) The Cunetio Treasure: Roman coinage of the 3rd century AD. British Museum.

Bijovsky, G. (2007) 'Aion, a Cosmic allegory on a coin from Tyre?', Israeli

Numismatic Research 2: 143-157.

Birley, A. (1988) Septimius Severus, The African Emperor. Routledge.
(2005) The Roman Government of Britain. Oxford University Press.

Bland, R (1991) 'The Coinage of Gordian III from the mints of Antioch and Caesarea', PhD thesis, University College, London.
(2014) 'The gold coinage of Philip I and family' in Revue Numismatique 2014: 93-150.

Boatwright, M. (1987) Hadrian and the City of Rome, Princeton, NJ, Princeton University Press: 119–33.

Boschung, D. (2013) 'Tempora anni. Personifikationen der Jahreszeiten in der römischen Antike', Das Bild der Jahrszeiten im wandel der Kulturen und Zieten, Wilhelm Fink Verlag, München: 179-200.

Bowerstock, G. (1990) Hellenism in late antiquity. University of Michigan Press.

Bowman, A. (2005) 'Diocletian and the First Tetrarchy', in The Cambridge Ancient History, Volume 3 The Crisis of Empire AD 193 – 337, eds. A. Bowman, P. Garnsey, A. Cameron. Cambridge University Press.

Bremmer, J. (2013) 'The Birth of the Personified Seasons (Horai) in Archaic and Classical Greece', Das Bild der Jahrszeiten im wandel der Kulturen und Zieten, Wilhelm Fink Verlag, München: 161-178.

Brent, A. (2009) A Political History of Early Christianity. T&T Clark International.
(2010) Cyprian and Roman Carthage. Cambridge University Press.

Burgersdijk, D. (2012) 'The Troy Game: the Trojan heritage in the Julio-Claudian House' Troy: City, Homer, and Turkey (J. Kelder, G. Uslu, O. F. Serifoglu, edd.) Radboud University Nijmegen.

Burnett, A. (1987) Coinage in the Roman World. Spink.

Butcher, K. (2003) Roman Syria and the Near East. Getty Publications, California.

Butcher, K. and Pointing, M. (2014) The Metallurgy of Roman Silver Coinage: From the Reform of Nero to the Reform of Trajan. Cambridge University Press.

Calomino, D (2015) 'Emperor or God? The Posthumous Commemoration of Augustus in Rome and the Provinces', Numismatic Chronicle vol. 175: 57-82.

Cameron, A. (1993) The Later Roman Empire. Fontana Press.

Cameron, A. (2016) Wandering Poets and Other Essays on Late Greek

Literature and Philosophy. Oxford University Press.

Capel, A., Markoe, G. (1996) Mistress of the House, Mistress of Heaven: Women in Ancient Egypt. Hudson Hills Press, New York.

Carandini, A. and Carafe P., eds., (2017) The Atlas of Ancient Rome, Biography and Portraits of the City, Vols. 1 and 2 translated by Halavais A., Princeton University Press.

Carlson, C. (1969) 'The "*Laetitia temporum*" reverses of the Severan Dynasty', Journal for the Society for Ancient Numismatics 1: 20-1.

Carradice, I. and Buttrey, T. (2007) The Roman Imperial Coinage, Volume II.i, Vespasian to Domitian. Spink.

Casey, P. (1994) Carausius and Allectus: The British Usurpers. Newhaven.

Cerfaux, L. and Tondriau, J. (1957) *Un concurrant du Christianisme: le culte des souverains dans la civilisation gréco-romaine*. Paris.

Champlin, E., (1978) 'The Life and Times of Calpurnius Siculus', The Journal of Roman Studies, Vol. 68: 95-110.

Charlesworth, M. (1936) '*Providentia* and *Aeternitas*', Harvard Theological Review, Vol 29 No 2: 107-132.

Christiansen, P. and Sebesta, J. (1985) 'Claudian's Phoenix : Themes of Imperium', L'antiquité classique, Volume 54, Numéro 1 : 204-224.

Christol, M. (1976) '*Panégyriques et revers monétaires: l'empereur, Rome et les provinciaux à la fin du IIIe siècle*', Dialogues d'histoire ancienne, Vol 2, no. 1: 421-434.

Claes, L. (2015) 'Coins with power: Imperial and local messages on the coinage of the usurpers', *Jaarboek voor Munt – en Penningkunde 102*, Leiden University: 15-60.

Clauss, M. (2000) The Roman Cult of Mithras (translation by Richard Gordon). Edinburgh University Press.

Coarelli, F. (1993) '*Note qui ludi saeculares in Spectacles sportifs et scénique dans la monde étrusco-italique*', in Collection de l'Ecole française de Rome, Rome, 211-45.

Cohen, H. (1880) Description Historiques des Monnaies frappées sur L'Empire Romain communément appelées Médailles Impériales. London.

Cohen, S. (2014) Transformations of Time and Temporality in Medieval and Renaissance Art. Brill.

Cooley, A. (2007) 'Septimius Severus: the Augustan Emperor in Severan Culture', eds. S. Swain, S. Harrison, J. Elsner. Cambridge University Press: 385-400.

(2009) *Res Gestae Divi Augustae* – Text Translation and Commentary. Cambridge University Press.

Crawford, M. (1974) Roman Republican Coinage (2 vols). Cambridge.

Davies, P. (2004) Death and the Emperor: Roman Imperial Funerary Monuments from Augustus to Marcus Aurelius. University of Texas Press.

De la Bedoyère, G. (1998) 'Carausius and the Marks RSR and INPCDA', Numismatic Chronicle, Vol. 158: 79-88.

de Blois, L. (1978) 'The Reign of the Emperor Philip the Arabian', Talanta 10/11: 11-43

de Grummond, N. (2006) 'Prophets and Priests' in The Religion of the Etruscans, eds. N. de Grummond and E. Simon. University of Texas Press: 27-44.

Dodds, E. (1965) Pagan and Christian in an Age of Anxiety: Some Aspects of Religious Experience from Marcus Aurelius to Constantine. Cambridge University Press.

Dowling, M. (2004) 'A Time to Regender: The Transformation of Roman Time' in Time and Uncertainty, eds. P. Harris, M Crawford. Brill: 175-187.

Drinkwater, J. (1980) The Gallic Empire: Separatism and continuity in the north-western provinces of the Roman Empire *A.D. 260-274*. Stuttgart.

Drinkwater, J., (1983) Roman Gaul. Croom Helm.

Du Plessis, P. (2015) Borkowski's Textbook on Roman Law. Oxford University Press.

Eliade, M. (1954) The Myth of the Eternal Return. Pantheon.

Elkins, N. (2009) 'Coins, contexts and an iconographic approach for the 21st Century' in *Studiern zu Fundmünzen der Antike*, eds. H-M. von Kaenel, and F. Kemmers, Verlag Philip Von Zabern: 25-46.

Elsner, J. (1996) 'Inventing Imperium: texts and the propaganda of monuments in Augustan Rome' in Art and Text in Roman Culture, ed. J. Elsner. Cambridge University Press: 32-53.

Ennslin, W. (1938) 'Philip the Arabian' in The Cambridge Ancient History, eds. S. Cook, F. Adcock, M. Charlesworth, N. Baynes. Cambridge University Press: 87-95.

Entwistle, C. and Adams, N. (eds.) (2012) Gems of Heaven: recent research on Engrave Gemstones in Late Antiquity *c. AD 200-600*. British Museum Press.

Estiot, S. (2012) 'The Later Third Century' in The Oxford Handbook of Greek and Roman Coinage, ed. W. Metcalf. Oxford University Press : 538-

560.

Estiot, S. and Zanchi, P. (2014) *'De Lyon à Trèves. L'ouverture de L'atelier de Trèves à l'époque tétrarchique et ses premières émissions : monnaies radiées et monnaie d'or'* in Revue Numismatique 2014 : 247-296.

Evans, R. (2008) *Utopia Antiqua* - readings of the Golden Age and Decline at Rome. Routledge.

Fears, J. (1981) 'The Cult of Jupiter and Roman Imperial Ideology' in *Aufstieg und Niedergang der römischen Welt'*, 2.17.1, eds. H. Temporini and W. Haase. Berlin: 3-141.

Feeney, D. (2007) Caesar's Calendar, ancient time and the beginnings of history. University of California.

Fishwick, D. (2002) 'The Imperial Cult in the Latin West: Studies in the ruler cult of the Western provinces of the Roman Empire' Volume 3 Provincial Cult, Brill.

Flower, H. (2014) 'The Tradition of the Spolia Opima: M. Claudius Marcellus and Augustus' in *The*

Roman Historical Tradition: Regal and Republican Rome. Oxford Readings in Classical Studies, eds. J. Richardson and F. Santangelo. Oxford University Press: 285-320.

Forsyth, G. (2012) Time in Roman Religion. Routledge.

Fossum, J. (1999) 'The Myth of the Eternal Rebirth: Critical Notes on G. W. Bowersock, Hellenism in Late Antiquity', in *Vigiliae Christianae*, Vol. 53, No. 3: 305-315.

Fowden, G. (2005) 'Late Polytheism' in The Cambridge Ancient History, Volume 3 The Crisis of Empire AD 193 – 337, eds. A. Bowman, P. Garnsey, A. Cameron. Cambridge University Press : 521-572.

Fraenkel, E. (1957) Horace. Clarendon Press, Oxford.

Gagé, J. (1934) *'Les jeux séculaires de 204 ap. J.C. et la Dynastie des Sévères'* in *Mélanges d'archéologie et d'histoire* 51: 33-78.

Galinsky, K. (1992) 'Venus, Polysemy and the Ara Pacis', American Journal of Archaeology, Vol, 96 no.3: 457-475.
    (1996) Augustan Culture, an interpretive introduction. Princeton University Press.

Gardner, I. and Lieu, S. (2004) *Manichaean Texts from the Roman Empire*. Cambridge University Press.

Gee, E. (2000) Ovid, Aratus and Augustus: Astronomy in Ovid's *Fasti*. Cambridge University Press.

(2013) Aratus and the Astronomical Tradition. Oxford University Press.

Geiger, M. (2013) Gallienus. Frankfurt.

Gersht, R. (2013), Herakles' virtus Between Etruscans and Romans, Scripta Classica Israelica 32: 201-208.

Gibbon, E. (1776) Decline and Fall of the Roman Empire. London.

Gillett, A. (2009) Envoys and Political Communication in the Late Antique West: 411–533. Cambridge University Press.

Gnecchi, F. (1912) *I Medaglioni Romani* (3 volumes). Milan.

Goldhill, S. ed. (2012) Being Greek under Rome – Cultural Identity, the Second Sophistic and the Development of Empire. Cambridge University Press.

Gollnick, J. (1999) The Religious Dreamworld of Apuleius' Metamorphoses, recovering a lost hermeneutic. Wilfrid Laurier University Press, Canada.

Gordon, E. (1983) Illustrated Introduction to Latin Epigraphy. University of California.

Gorrie, C. (2002) 'The Severan building programme and the Secular Games', in Athenaeum 90: 461 – 481.

(2007) 'The Restoration of the Porticus Octaviae and Severan Imperial Policy' in Greece & Rome Second Series, Vol. 54, No. 1 (Apr., 2007), pp. 1-17. Cambridge University Press.

(1997) The Building Programme of Septimius Severus in the City of Rome, Doctoral Thesis, University of British Columbia.

Grandvallet, C. (2006) '*Marinianus, successeur désigné de Gallien ?*', *L'antiquité classique*, Vol. 75 Numéro 1 : 33-141.

Grant, M. (1950) Roman Anniversary Issues. Cambridge University Press.

Gross, M. (1945) 'Literary Purposes of the Myth of the Golden Age.' MA thesis. Loyola University, Chicago.

Grünewald, T. (1999) Bandits in the Roman Empire: Myth and Reality - Historical Underbelly. Routledge.

Habinek, T. (2005) *The World of Roman Song: From Ritualized Speech to Social Order.* John Hopkins University Press.

Hansen, W. (1996) Phlegon of Tralles' Book of Marvels. University of Exeter Press.

Hardie, P. (1986) Virgil's Imperium: Cosmos and Imperium. Oxford University Press.

Hedlund, R. (2008) 'Achieved Nothing Worthy of memory' – Coinage and

Authority in the Roman Empire c AD 260-295. University of Uppsala.

Hekster, O. (2002) Commodu*s: An Emperor at the Crossroads*. Amsterdam.

Hekster, O. and Rich, J. (2006) 'Octavian and the thunderbolt: The temple of *apollo palatinus* and roman traditions of temple building', The Classical Quarterly, Cambridge University Press: 149-168.

Hekster, O. and Zair, N. (2008) Rome and Its Empire, *AD 193-284*. Edinburgh University Press.

Hemelrijk, E. (1999) Educated Women in the Roman Elite from Cornelia to Julia Domna. Routledge.

Henig, M. (1986) 'Caracalla as Hercules? A new cameo from South Shields', Antiquaries Journal 66: 378-80.

Hijmans, S. (2009) Sol – The Sun in the Art and Religions of Rome. University of Groningen.

Hill, P. (1964) 'Notes on the coinage of Septimius Severus and his family AD 193-217', Numismatic Chronicle 4: 169-188.

Hollard, D. and Lòpez, S. (2014*) Le Chrisme et le Phénix, Images monétaires et mutations idéologiques au IVe siècle*. Ausonius.

Hölleskamp, K. (2004*) Senatus populusque Romanus: Dir Politische Kultur der Republik – Dimensionen und Deutungen*. Stuttgart.

Holliday, P. (1990) 'Time, History and Ritual on the Ara Pacis Augustae', The Art Bulletin (College Art Association) Vol. 72 no 4: 542-557.

Howgego, C. (2005) 'Coinage and Identity in the Roman Provinces' in Coinage and Identity in the Roman Provinces, eds. C. Howgego, V. Heuchert, and A. Burnett. Oxford University Press: 1-18.

Johnston, S., ed. (2004) Religions of the Ancient World: A Guide. Harvard University Press.

Johnstone, P (1980) Vergil's Agricultural Golden Age: A Study of the Georgics. Brill.

Keizer, H. (1999) Life Time Entirety, a study of Aion in Greek Literature and Philosophy, the Septuagint and Philo. Amsterdam.

Kemezis, A. (2014) Greek Narratives of the Roman Empire under the Severans. Cambridge University Press.

Kennedy, D., (1992) 'Augustan and anti-Augustan: Reflections on Terms of reference' in Roman Poetry and Propaganda in the Age of Augustus, ed. A Powell, Bristol: 26-58.

Kool, R. (2016) 'A hoard of Antoniniani from Qula', 'Atiquot '84: 69-113.

Krmnicek, S. and Elkins, N. (2014) 'Dinosaurs, Cocks and Coins: and introduction to Art in the Round' in Art in the Round, new approaches to Ancient Coin Iconography, eds. S. Krmnicek, and N. Elkins. Verlag Marie Leidorf Gmbh: 7-22.

La Rocca, E. (1984) *L'eta d'oro di Cleopatra: Indagine Sulla Tazza Farnese*. L'Erma di Bretschneider. Rome.

Lamberton, R. (1983) Porphyry on the Cave of the Nymphs. New York.

Lamp, K. (2013) *A* City of Marble, the Rhetoric of Augustan Rome. University of South Carolina Press.

Lane-Fox, R. (1986) Pagans and Christians in the Mediterranean World from the second century AD to the Conversion of Constantine. Penguin.

Langford, J. (2013) Maternal Megalomania, Julia Domna and the Imperial Politics of Motherhood. Johns Hopkins University Press, Baltimore.

Lépaulle, E. (1883) *Note sur l'atelier monétaire de Lyon à l'époque sur la réforme de Dioclétian à propos d'une trouvaille faite à Lancié en 1880*. Lyons.

Leadbetter, B. (2009) *Galerius and the Will of Diocletian*. Routledge.

Levi, D. (1944) 'Aion', in Hesperia: The Journal of the American School of Classical Studies at Athens, Vol. 13 no. 4: 269-314.

Levick, B. (2007) Julia Domna Syrian Empress. Routledge.
       (2014) Faustina I and II, Imperial women of the Golden Age. Oxford University Press.

Liebeschuetz, J. (1979) Continuity and Change in Roman Religion. Oxford University Press.

Lipka, M. (2009) Roman Gods: a conceptual approach. Brill

Lo Cascio, E. (2005) 'The Government and Administration of the Empire in the Central Decades of the Third Century' in The Cambridge Ancient History, Volume 3 The Crisis of Empire AD 193-337, eds. A. Bowman, P. Garnsey, A. Cameron. Cambridge University Press: 156-169.

Lovatt, H. (2016) 'Flavian Spectacle: Paradox and Wonder' *in A Companion to the Flavian Age of Imperial Rome*, ed. A Zizzos. Wiley Blackwell: 361-375.

Luke, T. (2014) Ushering in a new Republic - Theologies of Arrival in the First Century BCE. University of Michigan Press.

Lusnia, S. (1995) 'Julia Domna's coinage and Severan Dynastic propaganda', Latomus T54:119-139.

Maas, M. (2000) Readings in Late Antiquity, a sourcebook. Routledge.

MacCormack, S. (1998) The Shadows of Poetry: Vergil in the Mind of Augustine. University of California Press.

(1972) 'Change and Continuity in Late Antiquity: The Ceremony of *Adventus'*, *Historia*: Zeitschrift für Alte Geschichte Bd. 21, H. 4 (4th Qtr., 1972), 721-752

MacMullen, R. (1967) Enemies of the Roman Order. Harvard University Press.

Macrae, D. (2016) Legible Religion – Books Gods and Rituals in Roman Culture. Harvard University Press.

Mairat, J. (2014) The Coinage of the Gallic Empire, PhD thesis, Oxford University.

Manders, E. (2012) Coining Images of Power. Patterns in the Representation of Roman Emperors on Imperial Coinage. Brill.

Marsden, A. (2011) 'An intaglio featuring Victory and Fortuna from Caistor St Edmund', Oxford Journal of Archaeology: 427-434.

Martin, L. (2005) 'Syncretism, Historicism and Cognition – a response to Michael Pye' in Syncretism in Religion- A Reader, eds. A. Leopold, J. Jensen. Routledge: 286-294.

Martindale, C. (1993) Redeeming the Text: Latin Poetry and the Hermeneutics of Reception. Cambridge University Press.

Mattingly, H. (1939) 'The Great Dorchester Hoard of 1936' in Numismatic Chronicle Vol. 19 No. 73: 21-61.

Mattingly, H. and Sydenham, E. (1923) The Roman Imperial Coinage *I*, Augustus to Vitellius. Spink.

Melville Jones, J. (1990) A Dictionary of Ancient Roman Coins. Spink.

Miguéulez-Cavero, L. (2013) 'Cosmic and Terrestrial Personifications in Nonnus' *Dionysiaca*', in Greek, Roman, and Byzantine Studies 53: 350–378.

Miller, J. (2009) Apollo, Augustus and the Poets. Cambridge University Press.

Mineo, B. (2015) A Companion to Livy. Wiley Blackwell, Oxford.

Morrell, Osgood & Welch, eds. (2019) The Alternative Augustan Age, Oxford University Press.

Moorhead, S. (2014) 'The Gold Coinage of Carausius' Revue Numismatique, 2014, 221-245.

(forthcoming) The Roman Imperial Coinage, V.ii (Carausius). Spink.

Moorhead, S., Booth, A. and Bland, R. (2010) *The Frome Hoard*. British Museum Press.

Moorhead, S. and Stuttard D. (2012) The Romans who shaped Britain. Thames and Hudson.

Mouchmov, M. (1934) *Le Trésor Numismatique de Reka Devnia (Marcianopolis)*. Sofia.

Nixon, C. and Rodgers, B. (1994) In Praise of Later Roman Emperors, *The Panegyrici Latini*. University of California Press.

Noreña, C. (2001) 'The communication of the Emperor's Virtues', in The Journal of Roman Studies, Volume 91: 146-168.
 (2011) Imperial Ideals in the Roman West. Cambridge University Press.

Ogawa, H. (1976) 'The Concept of Time in the Mithraic Mysteries' in *The Study of Time III*. New York: 658-682.

O'Mara, P. (2003) 'Censorinus, the Sothic Cycle, and Calendar Year One in Ancient Egypt: The Epistemological Problem', Journal of Near Eastern Studies Vol. 62, No. 1: 17-26.

Oster, E. (2013) Seven Congregations in a Roman Crucible: A Commentary on Revelation 1-3. Wipf and Stock.

Ousager, A. (2004) Plotinus on Selfhood, Freedom and Politics. Aarhus University Press.

Owen Lee, M. (1996) Virgil as Orpheus, a study of the Georgics. State University of New York Press.

Parrish, D. (1995) 'The mosaic of Aion and the Seasons from Haïdra (Tunisia): an interpretation of its meaning and importance', *Antiquité Tardive*, 3: 167-191.

Pighi, J. (1941) *De Ludis Saecularibus. Società editrice 'Vita e pensiero'* Milan.

Poe, J.P. (1984) 'The Secular Games, the Aventine, and the Pomerium in the Campus Martius' in Classical Antiquity, Vol. 3, No. 1 (Apr., 1984), pp. 57-81, University of California

Pohlsander, H. (1980) 'Philip the Arab and Christianity', *Historia Zeitschrift für Alte Geschichte*, Bd. 29, H 4: 463-473.

Poletti, B. (2018) 'Foreign Cults at Rome at the Turn of the Principate' Acta *Antiqua Academiae Scientarum Hungaricae* 58: 549-569.

Pollini, J. (1992) 'The Tazza Farnese: *Augusto Imperatore -Redeunt Saturnia Regna!*' in American Journal of Archaeology, Vol. 96, No. 2: 283-300.

Potter, D. (1990) Prophecy and History in the Crisis of the Roman Empire, a Historical commentary on the Thirteenth Sybilline Oracle. Oxford University Press.

(2004) The Roman Empire at Bay. Routledge.

Quet, M-H. (2000) *'Le Triptolème de la Mosaique dite Aion et l'affirmation identitaire hellène'*, *L'Institut français du Proche-Orient*, Syria, T.77: 181-200.

Rantala, J. (2009) 'Mother(s) of the Golden Age: Female Roles in the *Ludi Saeculares* of AD 204' in *In Memoriam*, ed. H. Whittaker. Cambridge Scholars Publishing: 157-153.

Rea, J. (1996) The Oxyrhynchus Papyri. Egypt Exploration Society, London.

Rees, R. (1993) 'A Re-examination of Tetrarchic Iconography', in Greece and Rome, 2nd series, vol.40, no.2: 181-200.

Rehak, P. (2006) Imperium and Cosmos, Augustus and the Northern Campus Martius. University of Wisconsin Press.

Roberts, H. (1998) Encyclopedia of Comparative Iconography: Themes Depicted in Works of Art. Ed. H. Roberts. Chicago.

Rostovtzeff, M. (1926) *A Social and Economic History of the Roman Empire*. Oxford University Press.

Rothman, M. (1977) 'The Thematic Organization of the Panel Reliefs on the Arch of Galerius', American Journal of Archaeology, Vol. 81, No. 4: 427-454.

Rowan, C. (2011) 'The Public Image of Severan Woman', Papers of the British School at Rome, Vol. 79: 241-273.
      (2012) Under Divine Auspices. Cambridge University Press.

Rupke, J. ed. (2011) A Companion to Roman Religion. Wiley Blackwell.

Santangelo, F. (2013) Divination, Prediction and the End of the Republic. Cambridge University Press.

Scheid, J. (1995) *'Graeco Ritu*: A Typically Roman Way of Honoring the Gods', Harvard Studies in Classical Philology, Volume 97: Greece in Rome: Influence, Integration, Resistance: 15-31.
      (2005) *'Quand Faire, c'est croire, les rites sacrificiels des romains'*. Paris, Aubier: 348ff.

Schnegg-Kohler, B. (2002) *Die Augusteischen Säkularspiele*. Munich and Leipzig.

Scott, A. (2017) 'Cassius Dio on Septimius Severus' Decennalia and Ludi Saeculares'. Histos 11 on-line: 154-161.*

Scott Ryberg, I. (1958) 'Vergil's Golden Age', Transactions and Proceedings of the American Philological Association Vol. 89: 112-131.

Scully, S. (1988) 'Cities in Italy's Golden Age', Numen, Vol. 35, Fasc. 1: 69-78.

Shiel, N (1973) 'The opes legend on coins of Carausius', Revue Numismatique Année 1973 15: 166-168.

Smith, R. (2000) 'The DECVRSIO Sestertius Types of Nero and the Lusus Troiae' The Numismatic Chronicle Vol. 160, 282-289.

Śnieżewski, S. (2007) *In medio mihi Caesar erit templumque tenebit*. The Concept of Octavian-Augustus` Divinity in Roman Poetry of the Years 30 - 17 BC': *Haec mihi in animis vestris templa*. Studia classica in memory of Prof. Lesław Morawiecki, (ed.) by P. Berdowski and B. Blahaczek, Rzeszów 2007, pp. 171-196

Sobocinski, M. (2006) 'Visualizing ceremony: the design and audience of the *ludi saeculares* coinage of Domitian', American Journal of Archaeology, Vol. 110, no. 4: 581-602.

Sommer, M. (2011) 'Empire of Glory: Weberian paradigms and the complexities of authority in Imperial Rome' in Max Weber Studies, Volume 11.2: 155-182.

Southern, P. (2015) The Roman Empire from Severus to Constantine, 2nd edition. Routledge.

Stamatellos, G. (1977) Plotinus and the Presocratics: A Philosophical Study of Presocratic Influences in Plotinus' Enneads. New York.

Stanley, F. (1994) 'CIL II 115: Observations on the only Sevir Iunior in Roman Spain' in *Zeitschrift für Papyrologie und Epigraphik* Bd. 102: 226-236.

Steinbock, B. (2014) 'Coin Types and Latin Panegyrics as Means of Imperial Communication' in Art in the Round, new approaches to Ancient Coin Iconography, eds. S. Krmnicek, and N. Elkins. Verlag Marie Leidorf Gmbh: 51-68.

Strack, P. (1933) *Untersuchungen zur Römischen Reichsprägung de Zewiten Jahrhunderts. Teil II Die Reighsprägung zeit de Hadrian*. Stuttgart.

Strootman, R. (2014) 'The Dawning of a Golden Age: Images of Peace And Abundance' in Hellenistic Poetry in Context, eds. M. Harder, R Regtuit and G Wakker. Peeters: 323-339.

Sutherland, C. (1937) 'An Unpublished Naval Type of Carausius', Numismatic Chronicle, Fifth Series, Vol. 17, no. 68: 306-309.

Sutherland, C. and Carson, R. (1967) The Roman Imperial Coinage VI: Diocletian to Maximinus. Spink.

Sutherland, C. and Carson, R. (1966) The Roman Imperial Coinage VII: Constantine to Licinius. Spink.

Swain, S. (1991) 'The reliability of Philostratus's Lives of the Sophists', Classical Antiquity Vol. 10 no. 1: 148-163.

Swift, L. (1966) 'The Anonymous Encomium of Philip the Arab', Greek Roman and Byzantine Studies 7: 267-289.

Taylor, L. (1931) The Divinity of the Roman Emperor. American Philological Association, Conneticut.

Taylor, L. (1935) 'The Sellisternium and the Theatrical Pompa', Classical Philology, Vol. 30, no. 2: 122-130.

Thomas, R., Editor (2011) Horace: Odes IV and *Carmen Saeculare*. Cambridge University Press.

Tomlin, R., Wright. R. Hassall, M, (2009) Roman Inscriptions of Britain Volume III. Oxbow.

Toynbee, J. (1934) The Hadrianic School: A Chapter in the History of Greek Art. Cambridge University Press.
    (1973) Animals in Roman Life and Art. John Hopkins.

Turcan, R (1996) Cults of the Roman Empire (translated by Antonia Nevill). Blackwell.

Urbano, A. (2014) 'Narratives of Decline and Renewal in the Writing of Philosophical History' in Religious Competition in the Third Century CE: Jews Christians and Greco-Roman World, eds. J. Rosenblum., L Voung, N. DesRosiers. Vandenhoeck and Ruprecht: 39-49.

Várhelyi, Z. (2010) The Religion of Senators in the Roman Empire, Power and the Beyond. Cambridge University Press.

van den Broek, R. (1972) The Myth of the Phoenix: According to Classical and Early Christian Traditions, (translated from the Dutch by I. Seeger). Brill.

Van Nuffelen, P. (2011) Rethinking the Gods – Philosophical Readings of Religion in the Post-Hellenic Period. Cambridge University Press.

Varner, E. (2004) *Monumenta Graeca et Romana:* Mutilation and transformation: *damnatio memoriae* and Roman Imperial Portraiture. Brill.

Vermaseren, M. and van Essen, C. (1965) The Excavations in the Mithraeum of the Church of Santa Prisca in Rome. Brill.

Versnel, H. (1993) Inconsistencies in Greek and Roman Religion, Volume 2: Transition and reversal in myth and ritual. Brill.

Vidal-Naquet, P. (1978) 'Plato's Myth of the Statesman, the Ambiguities of the Golden Age and of History', The Journal of Hellenic Studies, Vol. 98: 132-141.

Wallace Hadrill, A. (1982) 'The Golden Age and Sin in Augustan Ideology', Past and Present 95: 19-36.

Walton, F. (1957) 'Religious Thought in the Age of Hadrian' in Numen Vol. 4

Fasc.3. Brill: 165-170.

Ware, C. (2012) Claudian and the Roman Epic Tradition. Cambridge University Press.

Watson, A. (1999) Aurelian and the Third Century. Taylor & Francis.

Webb, P. (1907) 'The Reign and Coinage of Carausius', Numismatic Chronicle, Fourth Series, Vol, 7: 1- 88.

Weidkuhn, P. (1977) 'The Quest for legitimate Rebellion: towards a structuralist theory of ritual of reversal.' Religion 7: 167-188.

Weigel, R. (1990) 'Gallienus' Animal Series Coins and Roman Religion', Numismatic Chronicle, Vol. 150:135-143.

Whetstone, W. (1978) 'The Saeculares coinage to commemorate the completion of Rome's First Millennium', SAN Vol XV11 No.2: 24-29.

Whittaker, H. (2007) 'Virgil's Fourth *Eclogue* and the Eleusinian Mysteries', Symbolae Osloenses 82: 65-86.

Wight Duff, A. and Duff A. (1934) Minor Latin Poets. Harvard University Press.

Williams, H. (2004) Carausius: A Consideration of the Historical, Archaeological and Numismatic Aspects of His Reign. British Archaeological Reports, British Series 378.

Williams, M. (2003) 'The Sidus Iulium, the divinity of men and the Golden Age in Virgil's *Aeneid*' Leeds international classical studies 2.1: 1-29.

Wilson, R. (2005) 'On the identification of the figure in the South Apse of the Great Hunt corridor at Piazza Armerina', Sicilia Antiqua 1:153-170.

Wiseman, T. (1995) Remus : A Roman Myth. Cambridge University Press. (2019) The House of Augustus. Princeton University Press.

Woods, D. (2012) 'Carausius and The Crab', Numismatic Circular 120, 2, 2012, p. 66.

Yarrow, L. (2012) 'Antonine Coinage' in The Oxford Handbook of Greek and Roman Coinage, ed. W. Metcalf. Oxford University Press: 423-452.

Zahran, Y. (2001) Philip The Arab, a Study in Prejudice. London.

Zanker, A. (2010) 'Late Horatian Lyric and the Virgilian Golden Age' The American Journal of Philology Vol. 131, No. 3 pp. 495-516.

Zanker, P. (1990) The Power of Images in the Age of Augustus. Ann Arbor, University of Michigan Press.

Zanobi, A. (2008) Seneca's tragedies and the aesthetics of pantomime, Doctoral Thesis, Durham University.

INDEX

Z
zodiacal wheel, 55, 111, 118, 121, 146
Zonaras, 16, 58, 71, 172–73
Zosimus VII, 1, 8–10, 16, 65, 69, 74, 79, 100,
      147, 161, 163